ROCKY MOUNTAIN HIGH

Also by Finn Murphy

The Long Haul

ROCKY MOUNTAIN HIGH

A TALE OF BOOM AND BUST IN THE NEW WILD WEST

Finn Murphy

W. W. NORTON & COMPANY

Independent Publishers Since 1923

For information about special discounts for bulk purchases, please
contact W. W. Norton Special Sales at specialsales@wwnorton.com
or 800-233-4830

Manufacturing by Lakeside Book Company
Production manager: Lauren Abbate

ISBN 978-1-324-07891-3 pbk.

W. W. Norton & Company, Inc.
500 Fifth Avenue, New York, N.Y. 10110
www.wwnorton.com

W. W. Norton & Company Ltd.
15 Carlisle Street, London W1D 3BS

1 2 3 4 5 6 7 8 9 0

In memory of Spencer Grogan.
He would have loved this hemp caper.
Rest in peace, brother.

CONTENTS

PART III: **RISKY BUSINESS**

ROCKY MOUNTAIN HIGH

PROLOGUE

The view was spectacular. The property, a few miles north of Boulder, Colorado, sat on a little rise with the Rocky Mountains a mile to the west and the Great Plains a mile to the east. To the south, 125 miles away, I could see the snowcap of Pikes Peak. In the foreground was an unobstructed view of the Boulder Flatirons, the five triangular and semi-vertical rock for mations that frame the iconic image of Boulder the way the Golden Gate Bridge does for San Francisco. "Flatirons View" was an oft-used phrase in upscale Boulder real estate talk, surpassing even "Bordering Open Space" as the pinnacle of desirability.

Much more important to me was the thirty-six acres of irrigated pasture where, in a few weeks, I intended to plant a hemp crop. Hemp had just been made legal again after eighty years in federal exile. I turned to the real estate agent, a prosperous specialist in Boulder County farm properties.

"He's asking 1.5 million?"

"The seller is very motivated. Make an offer."

"What will he take?"

"The only way I ever answer that question is to say I know he'll take 1.5."

"I'll offer 1.2."

"I'll let him know."

I'd been researching hemp for the past year. I had read that growing hemp could clear over $100,000 an acre. Thirty-six acres times $100K is big money. The farm was obviously underpriced, but I was told the seller wanted out for personal reasons. I thought all the small farms around here, like this one, with irrigation and water rights, were underpriced. My reasoning was that the real estate brokers, who play a big role in setting asking prices, hadn't yet factored in the hemp multiplier. Farm sellers, mostly older folks who'd spent their lives flirting with the breadline growing corn, hay, or alfalfa, didn't know much about hemp, and what they thought they knew they didn't like one bit. To them hemp wasn't a real crop; it was marijuana, and farmers growing hemp were dope dealers.

On the buyer side, hemp wasn't in the mix yet either. Demand for thirty-six acres of farmland around here was pretty thin unless you had horses and were already wealthy. It was too small a spread to scrape a living growing corn and too large to manage without expensive equipment. The idea of buying a small farm in Colorado to make money actually growing something on it had been moribund since about 1900. My view was that the marketplace hadn't yet twigged to the emerging reality of hemp cultivation. But *I* had. Time to start a new business! I'd been starting businesses since my teens and had done pretty well. Well enough, at least, to make a serious bid on a million-dollar farm property. Hemp was going to hit the big time and I was more excited than I'd been for years.

I'd moved to Colorado fifteen years earlier from the East Coast, and I mean *really* East Coast. I lived for twenty years on Nantucket Island, which is even east of Boston, and I lived at the eastern edge of the island in a little village called Siasconset. Local legend has it you can see all the way to Portugal on a clear day. I'm so East Coast I was elected chairman of the Nantucket Board of Selectmen, a seventeenth-century vestige of Puritan democracy, sort of equivalent to mayor.

I traded in Nantucket for Boulder and never regretted it. For most of my time in Boulder I lived in the posh Mapleton Hill neighborhood in a downmarket rental. I have a nose for the best side of town, having spent a different twenty years as a long-haul trucker for a fancy van line. I've seen thousands of neighborhoods and can tell with a sniff and a glance where money likes to insulate itself. Mapleton Hill is right next to downtown, and I could walk or bike anywhere.

Boulder is one of the most beautiful cities in the country and was a great place to land. Even back then it was suffering from its own popularity, which has been one of the patterns of my life. I grew up in Greenwich, Connecticut, before it was overrun by the hedge fund boys, and moved to Nantucket before it was overrun by the hedge fund boys, and moved to Boulder *while* it was being overrun by the hedge fund boys. I'm not sure if I'm the canary in the coal mine or part of the problem. Probably the latter, but I'm no hedge fund boy. I could have been. I was handed all the advantages my town of origin, contacts, education, and attitude could provide.

Naturally all that Greenwich privilege was dressed down in ripped jeans, flannel shirts, and long hair, and called a meritocracy.

Even as a teenager I saw it for the fraud it was and wanted out. I got out. I got way out. My guardian angel turned me into a long-haul mover, so instead of croquet weekends, I was transporting my former classmates' belongings between Hobe Sound, Aiken, Middleburg, Belle Haven, Friday Harbor, Quidnet, and Atherton. If those place names don't ring a bell, it's because you haven't been given the frequency to hear it. Really massive money operates like a black hole; it accumulates everything and emits nothing. Places like Vail, Monte Carlo, Palm Beach, Malibu, and Miami are for the arrivistes. Massive money is content for the philistines inhabiting those locales to take the spotlight. Anyone who's read Michael Pollan understands that corn became the most successful plant on the planet by a subtle and patient manipulation of *Homo sapiens*. Money does the same thing: it thrives by moving between hosts, allowing the current host to hold the conceit that it controls the money, until it doesn't. Then the money moves on, unscathed.

Boulder, Colorado, is another of these money vortexes. As Coloradans not living in Boulder will tell you, it's neither Colorado nor the Wild West. They'd probably describe it as a redoubt of the Upper West Side of Manhattan or maybe a Summit, New Jersey, without Republicans. I don't get involved in those kinds of quarrels, but I did feel I was missing out on the West. I wanted a change and needed to make a living. I figured the best way to do those and get Western was to be either a rancher or a farmer. The looming hemp revolution made farming look like an easy layup, ergo my offer for the farm. The farm house itself was a horrific rectangular box that dragged down nearby real estate values. It looked like a Walgreen's plopped onto the prairie, with an interior flair reminiscent of an airport Marriott. If a key real estate strategy is to buy the worst house in a great neighborhood, I had that covered. The possibilities were endless, though. With hemp profits I'd pay off the whopping mortgage year one, and enjoy a steady income in the following years. I'd fix up the house, maybe build a nice barn. Get a few llamas, goats, a burro or two. With all that hemp money, I could move a clapboard farmhouse here from Connecticut. Get a barn from upstate New York or Pennsylvania. Yeah! One of those granite barns the Amish have, or maybe a giant red one from a struggling dairy farmer in Vermont. The only hitch seemed to be that others were starting to figure out hemp, too, so I figured I'd better hurry before they got on board.

Hemp is Mother Earth's super-plant—and I'm referring here to the industrial hemp plant, *not* the marijuana plant. It can grow almost anywhere and used to be a major crop. George Washington mainly grew hemp at Mount Vernon. In recent years, herbal practitioners have been singing from the rooftops that the oil from hemp, cannabidiol (CBD), can cure anything from arthritis to cancer. God's green Earth had hemp hiding in plain sight, but we hadn't *seen*. Now we had. Hemp was going to put all those nasty pharmaceutical companies right out of business, and well past time too. The War on Drugs against hemp was waning, and science was going to show us the way.

As any hemp evangelist will tell you, there are at least 25,000 uses for the plant. The main ones everyone talked about were medical, health, textiles, building material, bricks, rope, paper, fuel, and animal feed. Apparently, there are 24,991 more. Well, the US just spent the past fifty years getting rid of its textile industry, exporting the machinery, pollution, and low-paying jobs to Asia, so that was unlikely to become a significant use. You can make bricks out of hemp, but they aren't certified in any building codes so it couldn't be that. There's hemp rope, which is at least triple the cost of nylon rope, and hemp paper, upon which the Declaration of Independence was printed, but that doesn't mean anyone wants to use it now. I didn't know anything about fuel or animal feed, but since hemp has been illegal to grow in the US since 1937, there was no infrastructure for any of these uses either.

Maybe there would be, and the hemp clerics kept saying it was going to happen soon, but it wasn't happening yet. Hemp was being grown exclusively for various consumer products involving the CBD produced by female plants, and for smokeable flower. CBD products are found everywhere, from anxiety relief to sleep aids to hand salves to seizure control. Smokeable flower means buds that you toke, like a cigarette or a joint, but don't get you high. They just transfer the CBD into your system.

Gone were the stoner white boys in dreadlocks. Well, they were still around, but in Colorado, lots of hemp folks wore lab coats and had PhDs. Scores of them had quit tenured positions in university biochemistry departments or research jobs at Big Pharma and started hemp companies. Most of these folks were in their twenties and thirties. I was a Baby Boomer, and not the only one, who saw the potential of hemp. Regardless of our being universally viewed by the hemp vanguard as anachronistic supernumeraries in the brave new world of what everyone was starting to call the Hemp Space, and endlessly derided with eye-rolling catcalls of "OK, Boomer," we had one thing most of our young colleagues didn't have: capital. Not human capital, not sweat capital, not brain capital, but actual greenbacks, in bulk, sitting in retirement accounts. Some of us were growing antsy about the performance of those accounts. We'd watched once mighty dividend aristocrats like ExxonMobil and GE get unceremoniously bumped off the Dow Jones 30, and we were looking for greener pastures. If we intended to spend our dotage in status and comfort downing diabetic-friendly daiquiris at the 5 O'Clock Somewhere bar in Jimmy Buffett's Margaritaville retirement village near Daytona, or playing shuffleboard listening to a Styx tribute band in Sun City, or driving our customized golf cart to the early bird dinner at a Cracker Barrel in The Villages, we'd all need to seriously increase our nest eggs. Loads of Boomers like me were getting energized by the investment possibilities of hemp.

It all seemed like a Great Big American Dream. Easy money, ride the wave, invest in farmland on the endless prairie. Go west, young man. The frontier holds endless opportunity. There's an American story so old it has gray whiskers, just like me, but no less compelling for all that.

West of the 100th meridian, farmers have spent a century and a half trying to make some money in what explorer Stephen Long called "the Great American Desert." It gets just twelve inches of rain a year on average, and that average has been declining. (A good nor'easter can drop that much rain on Boston in a couple of days.) Sugar beets, corn, alfalfa, cattle: they've all been tried and never amounted to anything much for the yeoman farmer. Decade after decade, what money was to be made was made, after some catastrophic losses, by Big Ag. The yeomen were left with failed dreams and bankruptcies. They moved on but were replaced by other kinds of dreamers. That's what I'd call the real story of the American West.

Many folks from back East might have an image of Colorado from a John Denver song or skiing. Well, John Denver wasn't his real name, and he wasn't from Colorado. Most of us here aren't. Skiing, at least, is a real myth, if such a phrase makes any sense.

This time, though, it was going to be different—and that should be the epitaph of every "go west" romantic who ever hit the road looking for El Dorado.

Colorado had become hemp central due to pilot programs begun prior to full legalization, and the investment dollars were pouring in from New York, Dallas, Toronto, London, and Dubai. The Colorado Department of Agriculture was enthusiastically promoting hemp. Their young and dynamic director was beating the bushes to the farm community: plant hemp and beat the cycle of bust and then bust.

That was the sales pitch, and it was a pretty good one; good enough, anyway, to pull me and a few thousand others into its powerful maw. It didn't hurt that I had time on my hands and missed the adrenaline thrill of a startup. In the past, I'd started almost a dozen different enterprises and maybe I jumped into hemp so quickly because I knew I was finished with driving big trucks and moving rich people's stuff around.

———

I started my first business when I was still in college. It was a poster collection consisting of pen-and-ink portraits of famous intellectuals that I sold to independent bookstores back when bookstores lined business districts the way tattoo parlors do now. My second business was as a trucking contractor and my third was a textile company that imported sweaters from Ireland. I bought that company while still in my twenties and have never bought one since; it's easier to start them, and at least when you start your own you only have the problems you created, not the litany of errors a previous owner has been covering up. It didn't take me long to figure out that the sweater import business I'd bought was an empty shell of nothing. It took me five years to turn it into something profitable, and I made every mistake a budding business owner could make. I learned, I hope, from every one. The big lessons were to never trust bankers, keep your inventory under control, hire a great accountant, never let anyone know when you're in too deep, pay every bill on time, forget about a personal life, and take your suppliers to nice dinners even if you can't afford it.

In my search for expanded product lines for the Irish sweater business I eventually went to Scotland, discovered cashmere, and started bringing that over to the US. This spawned real success and, ultimately, I became the cashmere king. That's not a moniker I gave myself, but it's how I was introduced by a colleague to another cashmere manufacturer, and it stuck. "This is Finn Murphy, the USA's cashmere king." My cashmere import business spawned offshoots. I opened several retail stores during the 1990s cashmere boom and created another trading arm in private label manufacturing. Cashmere scarves by Ralph Lauren, Burberry, Brooks Brothers and many others passed in one form or another through my hands. It was an amazing transition for a former truck driver, and I enjoyed every minute of it.

Since then, I'd done several more enterprises. On the high end, I opened another retail store, where my suppliers included Oscar de la Renta and Valentino. On the low end, I was a consultant for struggling warehouse companies optimizing space usage in the Brooklyn docklands. I've done pop-up stores, pest control, and politics. None were quite as successful as the cashmere business, but there were no failures either. I write all this not as self-aggrandizement but to provide my bona fides. I knew what I was doing when it came to business and I knew startups. I was no Warren Buffett, just a competent business operator like millions of others out there whom I consider my band of brothers and sisters in a way Mr. Buffett isn't. We're not superstars. We're the solid utility infielder, good every now and then for the clutch single or the timely tag. We know what we are and are mostly fine with that but always, in the background, there's the lurking hope, ambition, desire, that someday we'll erupt into the bright sunshine and forge a monumental success. That takes more than just hard work and focus and a great idea. It also includes a good helping of dumb luck.

All my antennae told me this hemp thing could become the big score I'd been looking for my whole life. I was ready, but I'd never gone all-in like I was doing this time. From a business perspective, everything I'd done before this had been practice for the big game.

The farm owner accepted my lowball offer. He was clearly on the wrong side of history and didn't know it. People without vision never do. It takes a certain contrarian attitude to bet on red when red has come up five times in a row. The math carries the same odds, but to humans it looks like black is bound to appear. Buying a small farm in Colorado to grow a cash crop carried the same kind of contrarian view but . . . this time it was going to be different.

PART I
THE HEMP SPACE

Chapter 1
WILD WILD WEST

"Howdy folks."

I'd quickly learned that this was the standard greeting in rural Colorado. It was conveyed without a trace of irony, in a low drawling cadence, not Southern and certainly not Eastern. Rustic, sure, but the undertone was distinctly and sincerely egalitarian. That took some getting used to for a guy like me, born and raised in Connecticut where greetings of sincerity and equality were often in short supply and irony carried a punch far beyond its weight. Like any acolyte of the Atlantic establishment, I could pun, palindrome, and concoct terms of venery with the best of the wags in my college dining hall. If you don't quite know what I'm talking about, that's my point—the New England art form in which vocabulary is a rapier that thrusts with cultural dominance. It's used to appear smarter than you are and to belittle those who don't know the imperious rules and esoteric verbiage the craft requires. It's an easy vernacular to adopt, as I just did, especially if you've been bred to it, which I certainly was.

In short, Yankee vernacular is the opposite of "Howdy folks."

Out here in the West, status is conferred through a different set of cultural norms. One of them is to establish your connection to the pioneer past. That's hard to pull off, since fewer than half the folks in Colorado were born here. Another status icon is to own your own ranch, tech company, craft brewery, defense contractor, rocket ship supplier, or yoga workshop. Any business owner, large or small, has some prestige. I liked the entrepreneurship piece a lot, but the Great American Dream ethos tends to overlook the vast quantity of business failures that ensue. There's a reason the word "dream" appears upon that mythic American pedestal. My entry into hemp carried a good dollop of the dream but, to be fair to myself, I didn't drink the kombucha all in one draught, nor did I swallow the hemp story in one bite like an avocado toast point. I had reservations.

The hemp industry, as it unfolded here in Colorado, never viewed itself as simply a commercial proposition. It had a messianic tinge to it. For example, the fact that the industrial hemp business was always called the Hemp Space by its practitioners reflected its origins in the New Economy, a term that connotes a different approach to capitalism. That sounds very familiar to a geezer like me, and hearkens back to different approaches to capitalism from the 1960s and 1970s.

To be sure, there were still plenty of counterculture vestiges occupying the Hemp Space, but those gray ponytails in battered Subarus were not the majority. The majority were millennials. Some wore the mantle of science; others, like Pierce Grogan, my nephew and partner in this caper, were simply looking to make some coin. Still others believed in hemp and hemp oil with a religious fervor. Few of these folks, especially the hemp apostles, viewed hemp's resurgence as something so mundane as an industry. Hemp was new, hemp was cool, hemp was a disrupter, hemp had been unfairly vilified by the government. Hemp had 25,000 uses, and CBD was a medical panacea. Hemp had lived through eighty years of a very bad rap, but its time had come. The folks most enthralled by hemp refused to call it an industry, like toothpaste or fast food. Hemp Nation wasn't a nation of shopkeepers, but a cadre of revolutionaries. They called it the Hemp Space because that implied inclusion, and they saw themselves as a more evolved kind of capitalist. I was happy to sign on with all of that. I didn't share the evangelical overtones, but I didn't see how that could prevent me from making some serious dough.

The hemp revolution in Colorado was not led by stoners. It started at the universities and the Colorado Department of Agriculture (CDA). Colorado State University and the University of Colorado Boulder have had serious hemp research going on for over a decade, with the support of the CDA. Everyone's motivation was to develop a cash crop that might reverse the subsistence farming endemic to planting crops on a rocky alluvial plain in a semi-arid climate.

This can be confusing, because Colorado was also the first state to legalize recreational marijuana, but these are two entirely unrelated constituencies. The marijuana initiative was spearheaded by folks who wanted decriminalization of cannabis because of the stigma attached to its use and the resulting legal ramifications. Ultimately, legalization passed in Colorado when the citizens concluded that the costs to the law enforcement community and the prison and judicial systems outweighed any perceived benefit in keeping it illegal. The effort gained critical mass when public officials, always trying to balance budgets in a state historically hostile to most forms of taxation, realized that the tax revenue from legal marijuana would be enormous. Hemp, by contrast, was developed as an economic lifeline for small farmers.

——

When I moved to Colorado, it didn't take me long to see that this was a very unusual state. There was an alluring mix of urban, suburban, and rural citizens not inclined to emulate the political schisms rampant elsewhere in our republic. There was a functioning two-party democracy featuring Democrat and Republican legislators who were generally moderate, pro-business, and had no problem working both sides of the aisle. It helped that Colorado was ranked second nationally in college degrees per capita.

That attracted even more educated folks, and when those emigrants arrived, they saw the value of agriculture, open space, and the desire for good government from farmers, urban dwellers, ski resort operators, colleges, and employers. They assimilated easily and this created a positive feedback loop that fostered mutual respect. There's enough right there to make it an attractive place without even mentioning the Rocky Mountains, four National Parks, and a vibrant Latino community; some families go back to the sixteenth century and can trace their holdings back to land grants given by the Spanish Crown.

I also came to love the enormous variety of ecosystems and topography. The state's eastern half is the Great Plains, and the southwest is the desert. In between are coniferous forestland and alpine peaks with snow on top year round. Anchoring everything are the two great rivers: the Arkansas, which runs southeasterly, and the Colorado, which runs southwesterly. And the state is big. Back when I was a trucker, I remember a call from my dispatcher. I happened to be in Denver, and he said I was to deliver a shipment to Durango and be back to load in Fort Collins the next morning. I pointed out to him that the distance from Denver to Durango was enormous—it would be the same driving time as from Raleigh,

North Carolina, to New Haven, Connecticut. He was surprised, as many Easterners are, when given such big-state illustrations.

The bottom third of Colorado is transected by the Arkansas River, which starts in the Rocky Mountains and flows to the Mississippi. It's the sixth longest river in the US and probably the one least known. It's important here because the area of Colorado south of the Arkansas was part of Mexico until the Treaty of Guadalupe Hidalgo of 1848. While Denver is as cosmopolitan a city as any in America, go south of the Arkansas and you're back in Spanish America. Head west from there, and you're in Navajo country. Head north from there, and you're in the Rockies and Ute territory, with pockets of Colorado ski country filled with beautiful and history-rich towns like Telluride, Ouray, Crested Butte, and Aspen.

Nobody in Colorado thinks twice about a four-hour road trip west to the mountains or south to the Arkansas. Fewer people go east to amazing places like Bent's Fort, a rebuilt trading post from the 1830s, when the Arapahoe ruled the roost and dictated terms to the palefaces, or the Pawnee National Grasslands, whose rolling knolls finally make clear how much fun it must have been to ride ponies mile after mile running down bison. William Bent built the fort he named after himself; he was permitted a trading license from the Arapahoe and Southern Cheyenne after marrying the aristocratic Owl Woman and starting a family. This was twenty-five years before the Colorado gold rush, and white people had to show some serious community solidarity, like marriage, to gain any status inside the powerful Native structure.

You could spend your entire life exploring Colorado and not scratch the surface.

The Rocky Mountains are very close to the major population centers of what's called the Front Range. The borderland between the mountains and the plains, the Front Range runs almost due south five hundred miles, from Laramie, Wyoming, to Santa Fe, New Mexico. The Front Range is home to an ancient highway, created by *Homo sapiens* eons before recorded history, though I suppose the footpaths are in fact a form of recorded history. They were trodden first maybe twenty thousand years ago by peoples on their trek from the Bering land bridge to the bottom of South America. The term "land bridge" is entirely relative, since the "bridge" was probably 450 miles wide, but no less daunting for that. The time-frame is currently a subject of great disagreement; some scholars say the footpath goes back much further, and some say it's of a more recent date. Anyway, Interstate 25 tracks the footpath perfectly; the engineers from the Eisenhower days simply followed the route those ancient travelers had already figured out.

The Front Range has been a population center since then, starting with the Clovis people, then the Folsoms, and on to the Arapahoe and Southern Cheyenne in the late eighteenth century. Everyone stopping here appreciated the mild winters, the availability of water, firewood, and forage for animals. Naturally, there was a lot of competition, meaning violence, about who got to live here. The Front Range is now populated by tech entrepreneurs, transportation specialists, Big Ag, defense contractors, and a solid but dwindling cadre of family farmers, and they're still fighting about who gets to live here. Nowadays it's done with dollars instead of clubs, but it's no less competitive. The median home price in Boulder is $1.1 million, and for the Front Range as a whole it's almost $600,000. I don't know what a family with two earners, one working at a cell phone store and the other maybe at a pet day care or a grocery store, is going to do when it comes to home ownership. Well, I actually do know; they're not going to be homeowners.

When the first gold seekers camped in what is now Boulder in

1858, they met the Arapahoe chief Niwot, called Left Hand by the Anglos, who told them to go away. When they didn't, Niwot tried to get along with the newcomers, and for his efforts was massacred at Sand Creek in 1864. Niwot left a legacy in his well-known Curse of the Boulder Valley: "People seeing the beauty of this valley will want to stay, and their staying will be the undoing of the beauty." He left an additional legacy—shared by most of America, where many place names are attached either to the first white man to arrive or the last Indian to leave—in the village of Niwot just north of Boulder. For the perfect contrast, I live in Longmont, right next to Niwot, which is named after Stephen Long, a Dartmouth-educated engineer who "discovered" and named Long's Peak in 1822.

Niwot's curse aside, I loved picking up all this recent history. I also loved the climate. It was one of the many great unexpected surprises about living in Colorado.

When I first arrived, I was shocked that the city of Boulder didn't plow the streets after a snowstorm, making a morning commute difficult. Before I could even draft a stern letter to the editor on the appalling lack of city services, the snow had melted. It would invariably be gone by the next day. Boulder County has over three hundred days of sunshine a year. The bike paths, of which there are over three hundred miles within the city limits, would once again fill with commuters, and restaurant managers would put out the sidewalk umbrellas. This is *not* the Nantucketer's experience grinding through the long shank of a New England winter.

Almost five million people now live on the Front Range, and the Rocky Mountains are no longer seen as a forbidding and impenetrable barrier but as a nearby playground. A typical weekend outing, regardless of one's age, might be the ascent of a 14,000-foot peak, called a fourteener. Nobody bothers to ask if the summit is above your level of fitness. It's *assumed* you're in shape. There are fifty-eight fourteeners in the state, and a common bucket list item for regular citizens is to bag all of them. These folks aren't extreme athletes. They're postal workers or courthouse clerks or furniture movers. In winter, another standard outing is a hut trip, where you strap skins onto your skis and climb into the mountains to grab some fresh powder while staying a night or two in a back-country cabin. You have to hump in all your food and beer in a backpack. These activities are considered normal weekends in Colorado. Other standard pastimes include heading south to the Arkansas for a raft trip through the rapids or soaking in hot springs outside Salida. You can check out the many ghost towns or take your four-wheel drive SUV and see some country for real that the Land Rover commercials show on TV. Try elk hunting, or maybe snow-mobile the bowls around Steamboat Springs. Want some down-time? Head to Crestone, in the shadow of the Sangre de Cristo Mountains, and you'll have a choice of a couple dozen retreat centers to soothe your soul. The name Sangre de Cristo tells you, without a map, that you're well south of the Arkansas.

All this may sound like I'm working for the Colorado Chamber of Commerce, but I'm not the only one who feels this way. People come out here to college or graduate school or on some road trip and, well, they stay. Young people. People with ambition, brains, and a far clearer idea of life–work balance than my generation ever possessed. These were the folks who formed the vanguard of the hemp revolution, and it was the oil from the plant—cannabidiol (CBD)—that got everyone excited.

———

The chemical structure of CBD was first unlocked in 1964 by an Israeli scientist named Raphael Mechoulam, who also isolated tetrahydrocannabinol (THC). THC is the stuff that gets you high and remains federally illegal. Based on anecdotal evidence going back millennia that the cannabis plant provided relief from seizures, Mechoulam and other researchers began scientific research on the effects of THC and CBD on mammals.

It wasn't until 1992 that researchers discovered a previously unknown physiological signaling system, which they called the endocannabinoid system or ECS. The ECS operates as a natural repair kit for an organism, helping to restore equilibrium when that organism is attacked by disease, trauma, stress, or environmental factors. The ECS identifies and fixes imbalances in brain and body systems using internally produced cannabinoids that "turn on" the repair, and then release enzymes to "turn off" the repair when equilibrium is restored. Some of the cannabinoids found in hemp plants are similar to those produced by mammals.

The idea behind the efficacy of hemp-derived cannabinoids is quite simple: if your endocannabinoid system isn't functioning properly, maybe you have an endocannabinoid deficiency and maybe the ingestion of hemp cannabinoids can boost it. This might restart or strengthen your body's internal repair kit. While not an unreasonable theory, endocannabinoid deficiency is not a medical diagnosis, nor has the concept of introducing plant cannabinoids to humans been scientifically established as beneficial. There is feverish research being done on this very subject, but they're playing catch-up since cannabinoid research was nonexistent in the US for eighty years. In addition, throughout that time, US foreign policy strongly discouraged any other country from doing cannabinoid research either.

Naturally, sufferers of chronic health conditions that don't respond to standard medical treatments desperately want hemp cannabinoids to work. So do the purveyors of CBD products, as well as hemp growers, researchers, chemists, investors, and doctors. Everyone wants people to endure less suffering. There have been many promising studies and reams of anecdotal testimony about the benefits of CBD on humans, but here's the bottom line as of right now: *Nobody knows if ingesting cannabinoids from hemp plants affects the endocannabinoid system.*

My own interest in hemp, I readily admit, came neither from the murky science nor from any altruistic vision. I believed a lot of people believed in the benefits of CBD, and I wanted to make money in the Hemp Space. I wasn't alone. In 2018, CBD sales were around $500 million, and they were projected to rise rapidly to over $2 billion. There were already thousands of CBD consumer brands, and the number was expected to double every year for the next several years.

For me as a potential hemp farmer, those growth numbers looked solid. Given the level of outside investment, local government support, and anecdotal enthusiasm, it seemed like a once-in-a-lifetime opportunity. Hemp had all the hallmarks of an El Dorado in Colorado, and I was going to be part of it.

I was planning to grow hemp for smokeable flower on my farm. That's different from hemp biomass, which is used to make CBD oil. Smokeable flower is hemp that has been dried, bucked (meaning the stalks and branches have been removed), and then trimmed into buds that look just like marijuana buds. You can smoke it in a spliff or put it in a vape pen or pipe. In Colorado you could buy hemp bud packaged just like a pack of Marlboros. It was basically unregulated and actually easier than buying Marlboros, since you had to be twenty-one to buy cigarettes but only eighteen to buy hemp bud. People smoke hemp for the same reason people smoke cigarettes. Smoking hemp transfers CBD quickly into the bloodstream, so even though you don't get high, you get the CBD.

Biomass, on the other hand, is hemp that has been dried, bucked, and milled to separate the CBD oil through a chemical process called extraction. CBD oil is used in tinctures, drops, gummies, and many other products. Hemp biomass can be further refined into what is called isolate, which is used in salves, gels, and various other stuff. CBD oil and isolate, regardless of the final product, are all used as agents to theoretically jumpstart the endocannabinoid system. Biomass is sold as a commodity, by weight, based on its CBD content. Lots of folks were trying to develop exchanges to trade biomass but hemp wasn't traded like corn or soybeans, commodities for which there is a transparent and regulated market. The biomass market looked more like *World War Z* than the Chicago Mercantile Exchange.

Almost all the small hemp farmers in Colorado were growing their crop for smokeable flower. Their reasoning was simple; the market price for biomass was $80 per pound, and the price for smokeable flower was $350 per pound.

If the market for biomass was post-apocalyptic anarchy, the market for smokeable flower was the stock exchange scene at the end of *Trading Places*, when our heroes corner the market on orange juice. You just picked your customers from an overflowing corral of desperate buyers. Nobody was even bothering to develop an exchange for smokeable flower. The year before, flower was in such demand that buyers were flooding into farms all over Colorado waving wire transfer forms or paying cash for whatever was available. $350 per pound for this year's crop looked firm, and if it dropped—even, say, by half—there would still be lots of profit at $175 per pound. It looked like a reasonable risk to several thousand Coloradans . . . and to many others in Kentucky, California, Washington, and Oregon . . . and to me.

Chapter 2
GREEN ACRES

My closing date for the farm was set for June 10. I decided early on not to apprise the mortgage broker of my hemp intentions. As a serial startup guy, I've never seen any advantage in giving too much information to bankers, and hemp was still viewed in certain hidebound circles, like banking, as a variant of dope dealing.

None of my previous business experience had been related in any way to agriculture. As a kid from the Connecticut suburbs, my idea of farmwork was gleaned almost entirely from picking up rotten apples under the fecund tree in our backyard and from watching episodes of the late-sixties sitcom *Green Acres*.

I had two immediate connections to people who were growing hemp. One was a gentleman farmer, an equestrian guy, who'd decided to grow some hemp acres for fun and possible profit. The other was a former marijuana grower attempting a transition into a less legally fraught enterprise. They were both helpful and encouraging but didn't know much more about growing outdoor hemp than I did. The 2018 Farm Bill, which legalized hemp cultivation, had passed only a few months before.

In Colorado, prior to this, there had been some experimental growers under special license, and certainly some illegal marijuana growers, but there was no central clearinghouse of legitimate hemp farmers giving numbers to a public agency like the USDA, or any other formal exchange of information. There simply wasn't any public data.

With a more traditional crop, a budding farmer could contact their local USDA extension office or the state Department of Agriculture office for information. If you wanted to grow corn or alfalfa in Colorado, for example, one of those friendly and knowledgeable staffers could readily tell you the average cost per acre to rent land, costs to plant, harvest, and transport, a range of likely prices at harvest, and loads of other useful details needed to make an informed business decision. Not so with hemp. The neophytes like my connections had no information worth exchanging; they could refer only to the optimistic sermons on the internet, most often delivered by "consultants" who launched web pages to sell their "expertise" after an hour in the Hemp Space. One fellow I later worked with told me: "We paid accountants, lawyers, compliance experts, and consultants to help us figure stuff out until we finally realized we were educating *them*. They collected fees from us while they were learning the business. We stopped hiring experts."

Unfortunately, people who had experience growing cannabis plants and possessed important information to impart, were, by prudent habit, reluctant to share data regarding costs or planting schedules, or even to meet for a coffee. I know because I tried. I tried hard. I'd never entered a business before without having some general idea of the cost of production. With hemp I was flying blind and didn't like it; it seemed like an imprudent way to launch. But the omnipresent talisman of $100,000+ an acre, plus the

CDA's cheerleading, plus the media hype, plus all the money pouring in . . . well, it created an irresistible gravitational pull. I had plenty of company in this enthusiasm. Hemp registrations in Colorado had more than tripled from the previous year and the area planted would grow tenfold, to more than 80,000 acres or 125 square miles.

The CDA was exuberant about hemp. Colorado farm bankruptcies, always an active business for local attorneys, were going through the roof, and farm incomes were going through the floor. The new governor had appointed a CDA commissioner who shared his bullish views on hemp's potential to reverse the trend. Though the CDA was actively encouraging hemp, they had no solid information to give to prospective hemp growers the way they could for other crops.

Information was certainly there, in other hands, but there wasn't much communication or cooperation. This was astounding to me and still is. I've learned since that this is typical of farmers in Colorado and maybe farmers everywhere. There is no local internet chat room of farmers with equipment to sell, rent, or buy, or services to perform. There's a bulletin board at the Hygiene Feed and Supply store, my local farm supplier, and it's full of business cards for massage therapists, acupuncture practitioners, and astrologers (this is Boulder County, after all). But I never saw one for a guy who wants a hay baler or has a farm service to offer. I live in a massive agricultural area with hundreds of farms within a few miles, but I couldn't find a used pitchfork without going door to door. I suspect it's somehow related to the bogus myth of Wild West independence. I was just looking to pay a guy to cut my hay, and surely some neighbor had a farmhand sitting around. I wanted to buy services, but the fact that nobody communicated made it incredibly difficult.

———

It wasn't always this way. I know this because there are dilapidated Grange Halls all over the Front Range. The Grange movement was a farmers' fraternal group that started in 1867 and was a political force well into the twentieth century. Their main gripe was railroad freight rates. Farmers didn't like transportation monopolies, and they formed the Grange movement as a political organization to pressure legislators. As an example of their early effectiveness, the Grange movement was instrumental in establishing the rural free delivery of US Mail. In the 1870s there were over 800,000 Grange members. The Grange movement always had a progressive side and from its outset allowed women full membership. It was also a forum for farmers to meet one another, air their concerns, perform collective action, and organize social activities. My local Grange, Altona Grange 127, was founded in 1891 and is right next door to my farm. I joined when I moved there, and my sixty-one-year-old presence brought the average age down by about a decade. Our Grange only had twenty-seven members, and its activities consisted almost entirely of trying to raise funds to maintain the historic building.

My vision was to bring all the Boulder County hemp farmers together in one room. The Grange Hall couldn't have been a more perfect location. A group of renegade farmers, hemmed in by outside pressures, banding together in collective action, in a historic building erected well over a century ago for that very purpose. Hot damn!

I wasn't too concerned about the arctic air from the hemp farmers I'd already tried to meet with. This wasn't me; this was the Altona Grange. My vision was to form a Boulder County Hemp Growers Association. I lifted a list off the CDA website of all the hemp registrants in the county and sent out a postcard for a meeting at the Grange Hall. There were ninety-six hemp growers right here in Boulder County. Old times were back! I bought a couple cases of Coors, wine in a box, and some cheese and crackers. I was thrilled when fifty-six people showed up. I did a little intro speech and then asked if anyone wanted to speak. Nothing. Not a peep. Not even a popping beer top. I knew people were dying to talk but nobody wanted to be first, especially among a group of strangers.

I might be a patsy in other respects, but I know all about public meetings from my time as a public official back on Nantucket. This wasn't my first rodeo. I had seeded several people to break the ice if the public comment portion proved stillborn, as they often are. Once things get going, though, the next challenge is getting people to shut up.

"Who are you?" said my plant.

"Me? I'm nobody. I have thirty-six acres next door and am a member of this Grange. We're all nobody until we get together. Then we're somebody. This building we're in was built over a hundred years ago by the same kind of people we are. Look what they accomplished. Let's talk together about our common needs. Where are we finding challenges? There's plenty of hemp to go around, so we're not in competition. I'd like to know from you all what the problems are and maybe we can figure some things out together. I'll start with a basic question: How many of you are growing hemp for biomass?"

Not a single hand went up.

"How many of you are growing for smokeable flower?"

All the hands went up.

"What are your other concerns?"

Then it began.

"I can't get workers." Loud noises of assent on that one.

"What do we do about hot hemp?" More assent.

"Why did the CDA take so long to issue registrations?"

"The 0.3% THC limit is bullshit."

"How much nitrogen are you people using per acre?"

"What do I do if my plants are turning yellow?"

"I'm farming my father-in-law's land and he thinks I'm growing drugs."

"How do we find male pollinators?"

"Who knows a good irrigation company?"

Now they were talking! These were all good honest questions, and the litany continued for about ten minutes. I had no chance to answer any of the questions, they were coming in so fast—even if I'd known the answers, which I didn't. The questioners weren't looking for answers anyway. They were mostly just bitching. The Grange building around us was emitting its approval.

I brought the question period to an end.

"This looks really promising. All the concerns you've brought up are collective concerns. We've printed a form to put in the issues you might want to address. Please fill it out. If we want to go forward, this Grange Hall is an excellent meeting place."

I was pumped, but I could read the room and saw the energy flagging.

"Help yourselves to the food and drinks. Be sure to put your email address on the form if you want to get involved."

This was just like a Selectmen's meeting on Nantucket. Once folks get going, they begin to feel their power. I always viewed Nantucket Island as a hyper-democracy. Every resident considered it their citizen right to accost me, or any other elected official, anytime, anywhere, and make their views known. I'd be in the grocery store looking over avocados and somebody would walk up to me and say, "Paid parking downtown is insane. Are you insane too?" It's a small town. I got used to it. It beats apathy—most of the time.

Given the interest and the number of comments and questions from this hemp group, I was sure we'd have traction. I put the email addresses into a database and scheduled the next meeting to officially form the Boulder County Hemp Growers Association. I had some help from a couple growers who volunteered to set the next agenda, book the Grange Hall, assemble a committee list, and put forward a slate of directors. All the usual community organizing stuff. We chipped in for some more beer, set out folding chairs for seventy-five people, and wired the Grange with a PA system so folks could hear one another. Seven o'clock rolled around and . . . nobody. We checked outside to see if we had left the gate shut and checked our phones in case we'd gotten the time wrong. At 7:10, two people showed up. That was it. I scheduled our third meeting at my house and only one person showed up. I brought him into my living room, and he asked where the beer and appetizers were. We chatted for a few minutes and then he left.

In retrospect, I think folks went to the first meeting to see who was there, noted whoever they were feuding with, drank the free booze, and bolted. I did notice a couple guys taking travelers from the almost empty cooler for the ride home. Clearly these farmers didn't feel like they had any sense of agency or collegiality. That mystified me. Back East, my experience in politics was that citizens believed power structures were malleable, and were quick to organize, agitate, and change things that annoyed them. My Western colleagues, for all their avowed rugged individualism, appeared hesitant to assert themselves. They didn't seem to have much in common with those redoubtable folks who built the Grange Hall. After that third dismal meeting, I gave up on the whole idea of a Hemp Grower's Association.

But I had cobbled together enough information to arrive at a key number I'd been very curious about that nobody seemed to know or be concerned about. What does it cost? Well, a hemp crop costs $12,000 an acre from seed to harvest. That was a staggering sum, heard nowhere from the CDA hemp cheerleading squad. (For comparison, corn costs about $650 an acre from seed to harvest.) It was so exorbitant that I decided to shift my plans and plant only twenty acres instead of thirty-six. That still meant an upfront cost of $240,000.

———

I was busy that May working out the details on a property I didn't even own yet, knowing I needed to start planting in June. I had the soils tested by the Colorado State University Extension Service, worked out an irrigation plan, found a source for hemp seed, placed orders for drip lines and pumps, and lined up labor for planting. The only thing I didn't have was a hemp registration license from the CDA. There were thousands of applications pending and the CDA admitted to a huge backlog. You absolutely had to have a CDA registration to grow hemp. If you didn't, they'd view it as illegal marijuana cultivation with intent to sell, which carries a thirty-two-year prison sentence and a million-dollar minimum fine—and this is in hemp-friendly Colorado. In Texas they'd probably just chop your head off and put it on YouTube.

I had already submitted the CDA's nine-page application for a hemp registration. It was a straightforward form but had some buried landmines. For example, there was a check box to indicate no criminal history. This was an attempt by the CDA to keep folks from the drug trade out of the Hemp Space. There was no background check required, but the CDA reserved the right to conduct such a check. I also ceded certain property rights to my farm, the most odious being to allow my property to be inspected anytime and without prior notice by the CDA or any other agency it deemed as its representative. I read that as the DEA or the sheriff. The form required specific GPS coordinates of the planting area and an admonition not to exceed the boundaries. Another section was the listing of the specific hemp seed strains I planned to use. Finally, I had to pay them $500 plus $5 per acre.

As it was already the middle of May, the planting season was almost underway. The CDA understood this and were working hard to process the deluge of applications. They had told everyone the turnaround time was forty days from receipt of application to issuance of a registration. They also knew the drop-dead date for planting hemp was looming. In Colorado, June 30 is the very last day to put in plants. Hemp has roughly a 110-day growing cycle, so June 30 puts you well into October for harvesting. Most planting is done by June 15, since that lowers the risk of being caught by an early frost. Of course, planting in the first half of June raises the risk of a late spring frost killing your seedlings. This very tight growing window explains much of the historic travails of Colorado farmers—not to mention the added variables of floods, hail, wind, parasites, fire, and drought.

I checked my mailbox every day and kept going over planting decisions and financial projections, but what I was really doing was filling time. I made a bunch of phone calls to the CDA office to check my status, but all I got was a recording saying if I was calling to check the status of a hemp application, to wait forty days. On June 15, a month after I'd submitted the application, I took what I thought was the radical step of driving the half hour down to the CDA office to talk to someone about my application. If this was a radical step, it was a popular one. All the seats in the lobby were occupied, as were the window benches, and a group was standing in front of the counter separating all of us from the frazzled staffer at the front desk. Every couple minutes she'd announce: "If you are NOT here about a hemp application, report here. If you *are* here about a hemp application, a staffer will be out shortly." There must have been thirty of us in there when at last a very young man appeared at the entry to the inner sanctum. He looked us over nervously, came all the way out, and shut the door behind him.

"Hi, everybody. I'm one of the interns CDA has hired to help process hemp applications. We're working as fast as we can, but we know it takes forty days. If you're here to check on an application, we'll only look at ones that are forty days or older. All I can do then is verify that we have it. I won't know the status of it."

That poor kid. Poor all of us. We all had farms that were shovel-ready and were waiting for a piece of paper. I didn't bother hanging around, since my application was only thirty days in. I seriously considered buying the seedlings and dropping them in the ground without the registration, figuring it would come in any day. I went so far as to contact my longtime attorney about it and asked what the penalties might be. I think everyone ought to have a longtime attorney. It's fun to have someone who knows your quirks and it's useful to pay a professional to identify various risks regarding future endeavors. Most of them never seem to follow their own advice in their personal lives. My guy did a little research and came back:

"Well, if you're caught, you're banned from a hemp registration for three years. Plus, there's a fine of $2,500 per offense. Here's where the risk gets vague. What's an offense? Is it one offense planting unregistered hemp on your farm, or is every plant in the ground an offense? It's unclear, probably on purpose. They have lawyers at the CDA too. You don't want to risk a fine and banishment, and you *really* don't want to risk $2,500 multiplied by 30,000 seedlings. This isn't civil either, it's criminal. Do not plant without a license."

"Well, counselor, I was just down at the CDA office; they've got application files lining the hallways two feet high. They've got interns from the local high school, maybe middle school, it's hard to tell, doing public relations. I mean really, what do you think my chances are of getting caught?"

"That's not a question any lawyer should ever hear from a client, much less answer. Go read tea leaves, fire up some sage, ask a taxi driver. They always have opinions. I don't. I have counsel, and my counsel is: *do not plant without a license.*"

"Thanks."

"*Thanks* does not fill me with confidence. I can feel your oppositional Irish brain turning over your options from ten miles away. What are you going to do with my counsel?"

"That's not a question any client should ever hear from a lawyer, much less answer."

"If you do get caught, I don't do criminal law. Even if I did, I wouldn't want a client like you."

"Sure you would. I'm a client who always pays his bills. That's not typical. But, just in case you were going to lose sleep over me, I'm not going to plant without a license."

Case closed. I do enjoy mixing it up with attorneys. They're the most fun when they don't mean to be. If I'd hung around my fancy college up in Maine long enough to have graduated, instead of becoming a truck driver, I'm sure I'd have become a lawyer.

In the end, I waited, and waited, and finally received my CDA registration number on June 30. But the ship had sailed—it was just too risky to plant that late. No sense in losing the whole crop to an October frost. It was the rational decision, but I was crushed.

I'd just spent over a million dollars to buy a damn farm! What now? I couldn't eat the spectacular view.

———

After a few days I calmed down and figured I'd make my millions next year. I did have the farm, after all, and not growing a crop wouldn't necessarily leave me out of the Hemp Space. I was sure I'd find other opportunities. As silent and remote as most of my fellow hemp enthusiasts were, I was still meeting some pretty interesting people. Ryan Lynch was one of these. He was the kind of millennial wunderkind you're always bumping into around the hemp orbit. I found him early on because I'd been told he was a reputable seed supplier. Ryan was reasonably open for a hemp guy. Not loquacious, but smart, polite, and extremely knowledgeable. He put up with my incessant questioning with grace. He'd started a company called Boulder Hemp, which, aside from the main seed business, sold a line of consumer products, including its bestseller: a CBD-infused dog biscuit. Ryan was growing a few hemp acres out on a farm not far from my own. He was about thirty and had a PhD in evolutionary biology from CU Boulder. Looking at him, you'd think you'd seen him on *The Bachelor*: tall, slim, and handsome.

For his doctoral thesis, Ryan had tracked the genetic origins of various cannabis strains back when cannabis was still illegal, and a good deal of his research was done off university grounds. He had to separate his cannabis DNA strands from the THC before he could bring it onto campus to use the gene sequencer. He was eclectic about his experiments and even imported hemp from Europe to compare with the North American strains. One of the things he noted was that hemp seeds grown for fiber, which was the European stuff, and hemp seeds grown for CBD and THC carried very different characteristics in their genomes. After he earned his doctorate, he took a job in Boston working for a company he described as "the ancestry.com of cannabis." Just like *Homo sapiens*, the humble hemp plant had traveled a long way with lots of collisions with other hemp plants, making still other kinds of hemp plants.

Ryan kept thinking about hemp seed and the possible commercial possibilities: if he could develop a seed high in CBD and low in THC, he might have a business. He'd seen CNN correspondent Sanjay Gupta's profile of a young girl whose seizures had been relieved by CBD, and hemp was just appearing as a cultural phenomenon.

Ryan's so smart and competent at everything he does, he could be anything. Certainly a college professor, possibly a champion mountain bike racer, easily an executive at a pharma company. But he chose hemp, and he was slugging away making his company work.

Further useful advice was provided by Larry Matthews, who was planting a ten-acre hemp crop not far away with a couple of partners. I asked him if he wanted some free labor, so I could learn the ropes, and he said sure. So that June I started working for him, watering hemp seedlings in a greenhouse he'd rented. Larry wasn't exactly a neophyte, but he wasn't an expert either since all of his experience was of growing indoors. His ten-acre outdoor experiment would be his first foray into traditional agriculture as opposed to hydroponic horticulture.

Larry had a pretty good handle on the seedling angle but, like everyone else, was hazy about the rest. I asked if it would help if I put some numbers together along with an organization chart. He liked that idea, so I proceeded on two levels: farm laborer and bean counter.

The hemp seedlings in Larry's greenhouse looked prosperous, as far as I could tell. Botany, to me, is a closed book. I can identify an apple tree in early autumn. As a college kid I never grew weed; I *bought* weed. Larry didn't care that I didn't know anything. I think he preferred it that way. What he needed was a guy to work the hose and not second-guess his methods.

I worked in the greenhouse watching the tiny seeds in the flats grow nicely until it was time to transplant the seedlings to the fields. I was tasked with moving the 15,000 flats from the greenhouse to the farm. At the farm, they had a machine called a waterwheel, which was loaded with the flats of seedlings. The waterwheel had two low seats, and as it was pulled down a field row by a farm tractor the seated laborers grabbed seedlings and put them into a rotating cup. The cup first made a hole, then deposited the seedling into the hole, and then finished with a blast of water to surround the seedling with dirt. It's an amazing machine and you can do about 12 seedlings a minute if you have a good workflow going. Of course, a lot depends on your row length and other factors like reloading the trays, but we planted 15,000 seedlings in four long days with eight workers. I was impressed.

It took only a couple of days to see the plants growing in the field. One of Larry's partners worked the hot and dusty fields every day in a wide-brimmed straw hat carrying a hoe, scissors, and a magnifying glass. There's a lot of labor in growing hemp, what with strict irrigation procedures, soil amendments—meaning fertilizer and nutrients—and constant hand-weeding around the plants. I decided to call Larry and the boys the weedwhackers; they were good at it. There was also mowing weeds from between the rows and checking the leaves for bugs, pests, and disease. It's all this labor, plus a dollar for each seed, which gets you to $12,000 an acre in seed-to-harvest costs for outdoor hemp. I liked doing this work on the weedwhacker farm, but going home every night and seeing my fallow thirty-six acres was a constant reminder that I'd missed the boat. I should have been working on my own farm.

Another grower, also in the neighborhood, was Billy Held, a hemp pioneer like Ryan Lynch. Billy and I had a friend in common, and as with the weedwhackers, I asked Billy if he needed help planting. He said yes, so I spent two days on his farm. He'd been growing under a Colorado state pilot program prior to federal legalization. This was his fourth crop. Billy had his own extraction lab and his own consumer brand called A Boulder Pharm. Like Ryan Lynch's Boulder Hemp, A Boulder Pharm was a completely legitimate hemp business putting out a real CBD product you could track accurately from farm to dropper.

Billy originally came from North Carolina and had attended CU Boulder. He liked Colorado and stayed, like so many others, and found his way into hemp from his landscaping business; Billy knew how to grow things. He's a salt-of-the-earth working guy who bought his farm in the 1970s, when you could get one around Boulder for almost nothing. Billy had his eight acres of hemp fields, a few sheep, and a dilapidated Airstream in his front yard which he used for storage. Unlike Ryan Lynch, Billy was talkative. He'd talk your hind leg off about hemp, but I was never invited to his extraction facility, and he never revealed a syllable about his sales channels.

Billy was a pioneer in practice as well as spirit: he wasted nothing, never spent a dime more on something than he needed to, irrigated his fields with a simple gravity system, and was a successful hemp farmer. Billy didn't use a waterwheel, considering it too expensive; he preferred to plant seedlings by hand. His seedlings were in those red Solo party cups, and he'd dump a bunch of them midfield and you'd grab some, dig a hole in the wet dirt with your first three fingers, squeeze the seedling out of the cup and drop it in. In truth, it wasn't much slower than the waterwheel and it didn't need any equipment. Billy's frugality was so well developed that he didn't even pay people to plant his crop. He enlisted volunteers, like me. We were a mix of folks who wanted to see how the hemp thing worked, crunchy retirees, even crunchier college students, and friends. Working for Billy was a pleasure, and I learned a lot. He's just a talented and nice person who loves the Hemp Space.

Next door to the weedwhacker farm was another hemp farm growing eight acres run by a thirty-six-year-old professional farm manager named Alec Solimeo. Alec's crop looked so healthy I wondered how he was doing it, how he was irrigating, and what soil amendments he was using. One day I asked one of the weedwhackers about next door and he told me they didn't speak to each other and mumbled something about a farm equipment dispute.

I knew nothing about that, so one day I went over to say hello. This being a Colorado farmer and a hemp grower to boot, I was expecting an icy greeting or maybe even a gunshot over my head. I was getting used to this general suspicion, but I never stopped being a friendly and inquisitive trespasser inside the Hemp Space. I'm sure a lot of folks found me annoying, but not that day. Alec seemed glad to have a visitor. He was a young forty with long blond hair, a dazzling smile, and an open, innocent aura. His pickup truck had a gun rack on the back window that held a fly rod instead of a shotgun. His fingernails were caked with dirt, and he wore a soiled cap from a feed supply store. I liked him immediately.

"I'm originally from Cherry Hill, New Jersey," he told me. "I took off after 9/11 and moved to Gunnison, Colorado, when I was nineteen. I had no skills in general, and certainly no skills anyone in Gunnison was willing to pay real money for, but I wanted a simpler and safer life. I started as a construction laborer and ranch hand. Talk about the Wild West, those Gunnison guys are absolutely beautiful! They still rope steers from horses. Yee haw!

"I got into gardening around 2007 doing community gardens and moved to running farms. I like integrated farming, vegetables, goats, chickens, some cattle maybe. Keeping everything organic and clean and diverse. I've no use for monoculture and that's cost me in career opportunities and income, but I still remember why I moved to Colorado. Gunnison is about the coldest place in the lower forty-eight. If you can do a farm there, actually growing something, you're a superstar. They say the Front Range is tough; dry, bad soil, forget about it. The Front Range looks like the Garden of Eden compared to Gunnison.

"My family had moved to Boulder, and my grandmother was dying so I spent a couple years setting up farms for some wealthy guys around here. I've always had work. I've never done any kind of sophisticated networking. I put an ad on Craigslist for Farm Manager. That was all it took. I met an Austin, Texas, investor whose family had roots in Boulder County, and he asked me to do his eight acres for hemp. I didn't know hemp from blueberries, but plants are plants."

I asked him why there were no diplomatic relations between him and the weedwhackers next door. I figured they'd be a natural mutual aid society. He screwed up his brow in bemusement:

"These two farms operated next to each other for a hundred years. They'd both been mismanaged and basically abandoned by their owners for a couple decades. Your guys and my guy bought these two separate parcels at almost the same time. Before that, the farms were essentially commingled. There was junk everywhere from both properties on both properties. I went over to your guys' farm one day and banged my shins on an old disc harrow in the weeds. I pulled it out, repaired it, and plowed the rows in my fields. Last month, your guy came over one day asked if I had a disc harrow he could borrow. I told him I had found one on the borderland between the farms and fixed it up. Not only could he borrow it, he could have it."

"That was generous," I said.

"Not really. I was done with it, and they'd mixed up everything on these two farms so much it might have been theirs anyway. It's been a hallmark of my life that when ownership of something looks like it's turning into conflict, I surrender. I just don't have that property thing and I definitely don't have that argument thing. In my view, I resurrected a 1960s' rusted piece of junk that nobody even knew was there. It works now, kind of. It has quirks, but it's satisfying to fix things. Anyhow, instead of saying thanks, your buddy got annoyed and told me to never cross the property line again. Then he got mad all over again a couple weeks later when I hadn't returned the discer. How could I return it without crossing the property line? He came over one day when I was gone and took it. It's too bad. They have nice-looking plants. I wish we could talk, but it's not me. Hell, I'd still talk, but I don't want to get arrested."

Alec's story sounded reasonable to me, but I had no idea what really happened. Whatever it was, it was perfectly aligned with the dearth of companionable intercourse I'd been encountering in the Hemp Space from day one.

To cap it off, a mile up the road was gentleman farmer Tom Ward. Tom was a friend of mine. We'd met at Ignite Adaptive Sports, which is a snowsport program for people with disabilities. Tom and I were both volunteer ski instructors there. He was similar to the weedwhackers in that he wasn't looking around for other opinions, but his reasons were different. Tom was sanguine about making his own mistakes, happy to pay for them, and prepared to learn from every single one. He was a lone wolf, like so many others in the Hemp Space, but he already had his own consumer product, called Hempward Farms, which was CBD for nervous horses. Tom knew horses, was convinced of the efficacy of CBD, and ready to put his money on the line.

All of these people were close by. I didn't have to drive ten minutes to encounter almost the entire spectrum of hemp growers. The one part missing were the really large growers out in eastern Colorado, but I wasn't interested in them. The smaller farmers were all growing for smokeable flower or to supply their CBD brands. The Big Ag boys were growing strictly for CBD biomass and that was going directly to the corporate extractors.

———

I was enjoying myself immensely and building bridges in the Hemp Space. The bridge building was slow going, but I was getting to know some serious players and increasing my knowledge base. One thing I learned early on was some elementary botany. Hemp is a dioecious plant, meaning that male and female reproductive organs appear on different plants. Plants grown for CBD oil need to be females, since they produce the flower which contains most of the oil. Male plants do not flower; they produce pollen, which when introduced to the female plant produces seed. Pollination is bad for CBD growers because the female plant will use her energy to produce seed instead of flower, thereby reducing CBD content. Seed is also bad if you smoke hemp because nobody wants a seed to burst in their face when they fire up their spliff.

One of the key tasks in bringing a successful outdoor hemp crop to harvest is finding male plants early so they don't pollinate the females. A single male plant can pollinate an entire crop and ruin it. This is a serious risk, and its mitigation lies primarily with the genetics of your seed supplier. You need to buy as close to 100% feminized seed as possible, though no seed seller can, or will, guarantee 100%. Even getting to 99%+ entails some tricky biochemistry and explains why feminized seeds sell for at least a dollar each and are grown by PhDs like Ryan Lynch. The reason they can't guarantee 100% feminized seed is that in rare cases, a hemp plant without the male Y chromosome will show up with pollen sacs. This is called an intersex plant.

Since one feminized hemp seed costs about a dollar, a standard fifty-five-gallon drum full of feminized hemp seed is worth several million dollars and is quite portable—a fact which does not go unnoticed by folks whose minds turn on the possibilities of making money in hemp without doing any farming work.

Another risk of a crop getting inadvertently seeded is environmental. Pollen from male plants transported via wind and vehicle tires can contaminate your fields, not to mention hemp plants by the side of the road, called ditch weeds, of which there are millions in Colorado. This was another reason my farm was ideal for growing hemp. It's right up against the mountains with a predominately western wind, and there were no farms to windward. The third risk is sabotage. Someone could wait for the right wind conditions and empty a bag of hemp pollen downwind onto a competitor's field. Simple, effective, and very nasty.

The task of going through 15,000 hemp plants with a magnifying glass and examining each plant for male pollen sacs is expensive, tedious, and vital. Laborers on the weedwhacker farm walked the rows every day in an endless quest to eject the frat boys looking for a quick hookup with the female plants.

I wasn't involved much in that aspect of the work, having

neither the knowledge nor the patience. What I did do was stop by the weedwhacker farm several times a week and share with them what I'd learned from my research on the market and financial side. I'd given them a cashflow chart in early June indicating a best guess that they were going to be spending well over $400,000 before they were done. They didn't bring up my projection in any subsequent meetings. The topic we discussed most frequently, sitting pleasantly by their irrigation pond and watching their kids frolicking in the water, was where, when, and how they were going to sell their crop. As far as I could tell, the weedwhackers weren't any different from the other growers I knew in that they had no clear idea of a sales channel. This was another key facet of the industry where the CDA, always pushing hard for hemp, provided little guidance. The CDA recommendation was to get a forward contract with a buyer at an agreed price. That sounded nice, but hardly anyone was offering forward contracts.

What the weedwhackers did have were legions of potential buyers coming through, many of them flying in for the day from other states. The CDA had a public database of all the Colorado hemp farmers with their addresses. I'd spent several days in June with the list on my lap, driving all around Boulder County checking out the farms and locations of hemp licensees. These buyers must have been doing the same thing. They just drove up to the farm and asked to see the boss. Somebody would show them around, and they'd look up and down the rows, nod, and usually said something like: "Yup. Nice crop. We'll probably take it all. Call us in October." Nobody was doing real business, like writing sales contracts, but it was encouraging to have buyers from all over the country saying they'd be ready in the fall to lay down real American dollars. I was present for several of these visits and was happy for the weedwhackers, watching them escort prospective buyers through their lovely rows. Everything was lining up perfectly and if scores of people were willing to fly to Colorado to examine hemp plants for ultimate purchase, it was clear that the outlook for the sale of the harvest was pretty bullish.

Everyone was seeing green acres ahead.

Chapter 3
EL DORADO

I was seasoned enough in business to see that the Hemp Space was a classic boom. I also knew that there's often money to be made in booms for the careful businessman. Booms are fun things to play with—if you've got a strong stomach, a few shekels to lose, or just don't care anymore about winning or losing. History is full of them and there have always been more losers than winners, though that fact doesn't make any difference to the participants. Some try to outsmart the masses by opening an enterprise supplying the boom, like selling shovels to gold miners. That might be smarter than staking a claim in a land with no property law, but when the music stops, everything stops, including shovel sales.

What a boom needs above all is a myth for people to latch onto. A myth is something we believe is true when it suits us while simultaneously understanding it probably isn't true at all. Truth has no relation at all to myth, which is why debunking myth with facts has no effect. Myth is Orwell's doublethink with a Panglossian cherry on top. The hemp myth was that it was a medical breakthrough, a textile revolution, and a building materials bonanza.

One of the many problems with myths is that while they can evolve organically within a society, they can also be manufactured. All you have to do is find some basic human yearning and tell folks a story that lets them believe they'll eventually gain what they yearn for. Some of those folks will sign on. It takes no effort, no will, and no factfinding to adopt a myth. The best thing about manufactured myth is that the manufacturer never has to actually deliver anything, so it can go on forever. A few of the myth top ten that have withstood the rigorous test of time are eternal life after death for me, eternal punishment for my enemies, and the notion that our sinful present will be replaced by a rediscovery of our former ideals which will usher us into a glorious new era of utopian magnificence.

There's a symbiotic relationship between myths and booms. Booms often occur in clusters, and certain regions specialize. For example, upstate New York in the 1830s earned the moniker "the Burned-Over-District" for its boom of religious prophets. Texans have energy, Iowans have corn, Floridians have real estate. Colorado is alone, I think, in embracing just about any kind of boom. Those of us piling into the hemp boom weren't blazing any new trails in Colorado. For whatever good it might have done us, there were thousands of years of Colorado boom history we could have referenced.

The first humans to cross the Rocky Mountains from Beringia onto the Front Range found a paradise booming with megafauna. That's a fancy term for exceptionally large, mostly slow-moving animals, not accustomed to wily predators like *Homo sapiens*. (The megalonyx, or giant sloth, was 10 feet tall, weighed 2,000 pounds, and moved, well, like a sloth.) The behavior of all the emerging cultures was identical: kill the megafauna as quickly as possible, eat them, and convert their skins, guts, and bones into consumer products that could be used or traded.

There's a certain starry-eyed viewpoint that describes the Great Plains before the arrival of *Homo sapiens* as a wonderfully balanced ecological utopia. That's a myth. We can't know precisely the fate of the denizens of the dozens of other wonderfully balanced utopias that preceded the megafauna, except that they too were annihilated. We can trace these evolutionary developments all the way back to the beginning of time and grouse about invasions of plants, gargantuan mammals, roaming hunters, bacteria, ice ages, and white European males destroying something that was there before. I've no doubt that 400 million years ago the amoeba resented those newfangled two-celled organisms who were ruining *their* neighborhood. So it goes.

Regardless of who got to sleep with those super-soft woolly mammoth robes—and no doubt the women did the hard work of scraping them—it didn't take long for *Homo sapiens* to wipe out all the megafauna in North America. In fact, if we think about how the Industrial Age, from about 1750 to now, has in a very short time fundamentally changed our environment through various carbon compound emissions, earlier *Homo sapiens* managed a similar feat in exterminating the megafauna in about the same time frame. Nothing to be proud of, of course, but we could call it the first Colorado boom. This pattern has repeated itself so many times, I think it's safe to call it Colorado's manifest destiny.

Let's jump ahead fifteen thousand years and meet Francisco Vázquez de Coronado y Luján. The myth is that Coronado was the first white man to explore what is now Colorado. That he'd now be considered a brown man says something about our shifting views on ethnicity. Coronado and his cohort of a couple hundred horsemen were gleeful participants in the conquistador boom operating on the myth that the resident savages needed to hear and convert to the good news of Christ's great sacrifice. Coronado stumbled into what is now Colorado while searching for the Seven Cities of Cibola, legendary cities of gold (Spoiler alert: there were none.) He did find the Grand Canyon, or it found him, which must have been a hell of an impediment on his trip north. He returned to Mexico City two years later with a remnant of survivors and his own health broken. He wrote to King Philip II, in no uncertain terms, that the vast area north of Santa Fe—present-day Colorado—was completely devoid of water, cities, and treasure. His report resulted in him being stripped of his titles and imprisoned.

Nobody likes a myth debunker.

The only lasting legacy of this and other early Spanish thrusts and retreats was the horses they left behind. They didn't do it on purpose. Losing a horse back then was serious business, but what with the constant conflict, starvation, and desertion, some of the horses got away. They prospered, propagated, and were eventually tamed a couple hundred years later by Native tribes who'd been driven onto the Plains from the northeast by conflict caused mostly by population pressure.

Horses were first used by these newcomer tribes as food, and then turned into a transportation and military system that was, for a very short time, highly successful. The Plains Indian horse culture was in fact, another boom. Regardless of race, color, creed, or national origin, there seems to be something in the soil (to borrow the title of one of the historian Patricia Nelson Limerick's books) which makes Colorado particularly susceptible to irrational dreamers.

I like to think that Coronado's seven cities of Cibola were eventually discovered, if by that we mean a brief prosperity fueled by myth and a boom mentality. These are the heavy seven: beaver, gold, silver, shale oil, molybdenum, fracking, and hemp.

The beaver was Colorado's first modern city of Cibola. Demand for beaver pelts was driven by fashion. Early-nineteenth-century men of a certain class in Europe and America simply had to have a beaver hat, the way plutocrats today must have a London house, a Panamanian bank account, and a family office. Massive fortunes were made in beaver pelts, most notably that of John Jacob Astor, at the time the richest man in America. Alas, French Canadian trappers had pretty much tapped out the resolute rodents by the late 1830s. That worked out just fine, as these things generally do, because silk became the fabric of choice for aristocratic headwear due to the opening of the China trade. Silk caused the North American beaver trade to collapse almost overnight.

Colorado's second city of Cibola was gold. It was first discovered just west of what is now Denver in 1858 by a Georgia prospector named William Greenberry Russell. "Discovered" is an odd word, since the Indians knew all about the gold in the mountains but didn't attach any importance to a substance that could be put to no productive use. The Colorado gold rush caused an avalanche of emigration quicker and larger than the California gold rush, but much less remembered in American mythology. The 1859 gold rush had a lot to do with the economic panic of 1857–58 and with the unrest caused by the possible extension of slavery to new states. The doctrine of popular sovereignty allowed any territory to choose between "free" or "slave" via plebiscite. The Kansas Territory, which Colorado was a part of at the time, became known as Bleeding Kansas due to the rapid arrival of pro-slavery and anti-slavery settlers who fought each other savagely. John Brown, of Harper's Ferry fame, fought in Kansas against pro-slavery forces.

Regardless of any Kansan's view regarding slavery in 1859, they were united in the boom possibilities presented by the gold rush. The dusty hamlets of Kansas and Missouri competed voraciously to become the starting point for travelers to the Front Range. Cities like St. Joseph and St. Louis in Missouri and Independence and Abilene in Kansas were all origination points for what was then called the Pikes Peak gold fields. These towns all sent out flyers and bought advertisements in Eastern newspapers touting their advantages.

Early moving companies like Russell, Majors, and Waddell consolidated these travelers into wagon trains and hired drivers to take the emigrants and their household goods across the Plains. The same company also operated the Pony Express, a short-lived and unprofitable business calamity that remains mythically enshrined in grammar school curricula. Buffalo Bill Cody and Wild Bill Hickok both worked for the firm. Had I been born in the right century, I like to think I would have too. (As a long-haul mover, I regularly filled a wagon with household goods and traveled across the prairie.) These early transport companies moved people, mail, and freight, but what Colorado needed more than manpower was capital. Knowing this, the town boosters in shantytowns like Denver, Auraria, Golden, Black Hawk, and Central City began setting up gold mining companies to lure Eastern money. They were eminently successful. Between 1860 and 1900 Colorado hucksters garnered over $600 million in investment while shipping less than $300 million in gold back to their Eastern suckers.

Silver was Colorado's next city of Cibola. In 1878 Congress authorized massive federal government purchases of silver for coinage. This law, called the Bland–Allison Act, brought another boom to Colorado, and established the cities of Aspen, Creede, Georgetown, and many others. It also boosted the building of railroads and attracted thousands of emigrants to do the work. Government silver purchases were increased with the Sherman Silver Purchase Act of 1890, with the deliberate result that the price of silver rose to the point where silver mining was profitable. But in 1893 Congress repealed the Silver Acts and the price of silver plummeted, leaving ghost towns throughout Colorado. The boom was created by crooked politicians who created a government floor price, and the bust was created by politicians removing it. This reminds me of the sage observation of Lincoln's first Secretary of War, Simon Cameron, who famously quipped: "An honest politician is one who, when he is bought, will stay bought."

The element molybdenum had two boom-and-busts in Colorado. The first was during World War I, when steelmakers figured out that adding this hard-to-spell-and-pronounce metal made for tougher steel. Molybdenum mining was the mainstay of towns like Leadville, Nederland, Crested Butte, and Empire, which grew fast—and fell even faster when prices collapsed in 1924. Molybdenum in Colorado had a renaissance in the 1970s and the mines reopened for a time, gaining international attention—especially from the Chinese, who were taught by the Coloradans how to mine and process it. The Chinese moved back to China and by 1980 the workers' paradise, another myth, had put the rest of the world's molybdenum producers out of business.

Colorado's next boom was fueled by shale oil. After the energy crisis in 1979, Exxon, in 1980, with the full support of the US government and the state of Colorado, signed a contract to invest $5 billion on the western slope of Colorado to extract shale oil from the unyielding rock. Exxon claimed the region would eventually hold half a million people, with solid jobs and great communities, and relieve America's dependence on foreign oil despots. In 1982, Exxon abruptly left, having found that extracting oil from shale was tough work. Besides, the price of oil had stabilized, and there were easier and safer ways for Exxon to get oil—like filling ships at Valdez, Alaska.

Colorado's penultimate boom, the hydraulic fracturing industry, or fracking, is now spitting up blood before its inevitable demise. This energy boom started in the late 2010s. New technologies in horizontal drilling, along with a toxic cocktail of water and who knows what else, coaxed the stingy oil and natural gas to release their bounty. This catapulted Weld County, Colorado, into one of the top energy-producing regions in the US in 2019, and helped make the US the largest oil producer in the world. That flow of oil and gas has not, however, produced a river of profits. It's produced a river of debt that was hemorrhaging long before the subsequent oil price shocks. I know a lawyer who works for a hedge fund. I spoke to him recently and asked him what he's doing. This guy, who wears a three-piece suit and works in a lovely office in Washington, DC, told me: "I'm a loan shark for frackers." At one point in 2020 the price for shale oil was minus $47 a barrel. I seriously considered driving over to Greeley with an empty oil drum and asking $47 for my trouble but decided against it. Just like hemp, crude oil needs expensive post-harvest processing.

And now we've arrived at Colorado's seventh city of Cibola. Hemp carried all the components of a classic Colorado boom: unrelenting hype, a steep increase in demand, rosy forecasts by self-anointed experts, large-scale government support, exuberant investment from outsiders, and a bountiful supply of emigrants and locals eager to ride the wave. That was certainly me with my million-dollar mortgaged farm, Ryan Lynch with his proprietary hemp seed, Billy Held, Tom Ward, Alec Solimeo, and the weed-whackers, all with our modest fields and big dreams.

I've left out other booms, and their accompanying myths, in uranium, craft beer, ski resorts, sugar beets, casinos, coal, railroads, gypsum, vanadium, and marijuana. It's no coincidence that all these booms happened out here in the Wild West. The frontier cowboy myth, phony as it is, is the lens through which all other American myths are viewed. After twenty years as a long-haul trucker and fifteen years in Colorado, I've lost any patience or affinity I might have had for the myth of the American West I was given in grammar school. It wasn't just grammar school either. Anything considered distinctly American is infected with this frontier attachment. Books, comics, movies, TV shows, politicians, advertisers, churchmen, bar owners, truck stop operators, college professors, cops, criminals, real estate developers, consumer brands, environmentalists, rednecks, and hippies have in their various ways propelled the equal-opportunity myth that we're all latter-day cowboys in charge of our personal destinies as renegade individualists. Any one of us can get rich, become president, or both, and all it takes is the same pluck our intrepid white frontier forebears had.

If a kid from New England had this mythical moonshine melded into his brain, imagine the pull it has for a third-generation livestock rancher in Colorado. The myth is a drug. Maybe another definition of myth is that it is an addiction shared by an entire society; like all addictions, the essential components are compulsion, impaired control, persistence, irritability, relapse, and craving. As a backstop, there is also intolerance of criticism and a rabid vilification of anyone who dares name it for what it is.

It's long past time this childish frontier conceit dies its well-deserved death. It can't happen soon enough for me. Truckers hold onto it because they've got nothing else. They want to be seen as Riders of the Purple Sage because they're broke and at the bottom of the economic and social ladder. The small Western ranchers and farmers are almost broke too, but at least they can stand on their cultural pedestal as the vestigial remnants of those individualistic pioneers who built this country. They'd be *totally* broke if they didn't have their lips stuck to the federal udder, which provides them with subsidized water, subsidized land, and scores of other subsidies from the USDA.

In return for all these goodies, many Western ranchers and farmers cling to their myth of maintaining a distinctly independent American way of life by transferring their complete reliance as welfare recipients into a visceral hatred of the very government that feeds them. As Mark Twain wrote: "If you pick up a starving dog and make him prosperous, he will not bite you. This is the principal difference between a dog and a man."

Most of the land in the West isn't even owned by family ranchers or farmers and never was. It's owned these days by folks like John Malone (cable TV), the Emmerson family (lumber), the Reed family (logging), Ted Turner (broadcasting), the Simplot family (McDonald's French fries), Ralph Lauren (fashion), Koch Industries (oil and gas), the Walton family (Walmart), Peter Buck (Subway sandwiches), and scores of other billionaires who use the ranch subsidies and tax dodges to offset profits from their main business holdings. Together these folks own over 40 million acres, an area larger than the entire state of West Virginia—and, of course, *all* the water.

This idea of family ranchers and farmers upholding some mythical idea of a primordial pioneer American way of life is a cancer on our national character, not least because it lets the corporate ranchers and Big Ag hide behind a picture of a ruddy man in a John Deere cap. It also glorifies bogus individualism at the expense of national action and community purpose. I see it every day here in Colorado. The more some rancher claiming to be a "real American" rants about a welfare mother in Harlem not being one, the more I can be sure he's getting way more from Uncle Sam than she is. One important difference is that the mother in Harlem knows she's dependent and probably doesn't like it. Many ranchers refuse to admit their dependence at all, and yet they do like it. They like it a lot. Their main complaint about the government they despise is that their welfare ranching payments aren't big enough. Their secondary complaint is that their horrendous stewardship of the public land under their control shouldn't be held to any account by their landlords. That's us.

Plenty of the younger folks in the Hemp Space talked to me about the New Economy and their lost faith in capitalism. They see inequality, cozy relationships between government and business, and two political parties that to them are indistinguishable, as capitalism. They have real concerns, but their beef is with corporatocracy, not capitalism. My seven cities of Cibola were all corporatocracies. Private interests requested, begged, or bought government intervention, promotion, and investment during all of those booms while simultaneously propagating a myth of self-reliance for the poor suckers who dug the ditches.

That's not capitalism the way small business operators like me understand it. I'm a capitalist to my very core. I relish competing daily with market forces. So does a Korean immigrant opening a bodega in the Bronx, or a Mexican-American in Colorado starting a landscaping business. We're fine with competition. What we're not fine with is enterprises buying representation in government to reduce or eliminate market forces. As the comedian Robin Williams once said: "Politicians should wear sponsor jackets with patches on them like NASCAR drivers, then we'd know who owns them."

———

By the middle of August the weedwhacker plants in the field were looking great. The workers were there all day every day with magnifying glasses and snippers looking for male pollinators. Weeding was another daily function, and the rows were beautiful. Some of the plants were more than four feet high and the field looked a lot like an early-stage Christmas tree farm. The aroma wasn't reminiscent of Christmas, though. That year, Boulder County smelled like cannabis all the way from Longmont to Ward—though, to be fair, Ward has probably smelled like that since about 1971.

As they got ready for harvest, the weedwhackers' biggest worry was how quickly their plants were accumulating the psychoactive and illegal THC. Hemp plants build up CBD as they grow, and also build up THC in a biological ratio. The federal Farm Bill that legalized hemp set 0.3% THC as the legal limit for a hemp plant. Plants over that limit were no longer hemp but marijuana. Hemp farmers call over-the-limit plants "hot hemp," while cops and federal prosecutors call them "felony drug cultivation."

The legal limit of 0.3% THC was adopted from the work of two Canadian horticulturalists back in 1976. In an article for the journal *Taxon* they wrote: "It will be noted that we arbitrarily adopt a concentration of 0.3% Delta9-THC (dry weight basis) in young, vigorous leaves of relatively mature plants as a guide to discriminating two classes of plants." I'm embarrassed to report that the above fragment constitutes the complete US government research on the issue.

What was certain was that the weedwhacker plants needed to stay below 0.3%. Every week they'd been paying a testing lab— another large new industry sprouting in Colorado—for CBD and

THC levels to make sure their plants were compliant. The trick was to determine a harvest date that would maximize the CBD concentration without popping over 0.3% THC, and send that date to the CDA. The CDA would then come and test some sample plants before approving your harvest. If your plants were hot, they'd order your entire crop destroyed—and that would be only the beginning of your problems.

Chapter 4
START ME UP

Ever since deciding not to grow on my own farm that first year, I'd been looking for some place to land in the Hemp Space and make some money.

I'd heard no chatter in the Hemp Space about how to turn hemp plants into smokeable flower. The first opportunity I'd looked at, outside of growing, was hemp extraction, which gets the CBD out of hemp plants. There are many types of extraction methods and hundreds of companies doing it. So many, in fact, that after five months of research, I couldn't nail down the ideal extraction process. The simplest method is to go to the basement and toss some butane into a glass jar with your plant material. The butane separates the oil from the leaves and is then heated off. That leaves you with the oil. If you're wondering about the wisdom of heating butane in an enclosed area then you're smarter than a lot of home extractors who, like meth cookers, routinely blow up their basements.

For serious commercial extraction, there are essentially three methods. The first is the solvent method using butane, ethanol, propane, or isopropyl alcohol to separate the oil. The second is olive oil, the traditional method, but not commercially viable, and the third is carbon dioxide or CO_2 extraction. There are other outlier methods, such as water extraction using steam, and new processes are emerging all the time.

There had been a critical shortage of extractors in the years leading up to hemp legalization. Many farmers growing under Colorado pilot programs had to leave their crop in the ground for lack of an extractor. In tune with the boom, extractors had sprouted everywhere following legalization. This happened in a matter of months and was impressive because an ultramodern extraction facility costs millions of dollars and carries all kinds of regulatory requirements too. Not a problem for the extraction folks flush with Canadian, American, and Emirati capital beaming into Colorado. They were going to be ready this time and make so much money they wouldn't have time to count it all.

I rejected the idea of doing an extraction business. The initial investment was far beyond my means and so was the engineering knowledge required to set up a facility and operate it. My list of opportunities was getting shorter. Growing was out, extraction was out. What I saw remaining was launching a consumer CBD brand or opening a brokerage house to buy and sell hemp in the marketplace.

It was a fascinating time in Colorado. You could spend seven nights a week attending seminars or meetups discussing where the money was going to be made in this new industry. I did that. I went everywhere and talked to everyone. As far as consumer products were concerned, I attended one meeting where a brand consultant said there were already eight thousand CBD brands in the USA, and she expected that to become twenty five thousand in three years. I attempted to verify that and, like everything else in the Hemp Space, it was unverifiable. On the other hand, thirty minutes on the internet would show anybody that the existing brands were fighting like cats in a bag to separate themselves from one another, which is why the branding consultant was giving the free lecture in the first place. A pattern emerged through my research. All of the companies were vertically integrated, all were using organic practices, all knew their farmers personally, if they weren't the farmers themselves, all had their own extraction facility, quality control, and the cleanest, best CBD products to be found anywhere on planet Earth. All those claims were almost never true, but it made a fine narrative. That was enough for me, I didn't see any opportunity in joining several thousand others in a consumer products race to the bottom.

Brokering was all that seemed to be left. That was also an education. Every casual former dope dealer who'd sold an ounce of garage-grown weed to his cousin was already in the business. So were the extractors, the growers, and the CBD stores, which were opening on every retail corner that had previously either been vacant or held a tattoo parlor or an immigration law office. Mortgage originators who'd been flipping burgers since the 2008 banking crisis were now hemp brokers. I'd be having breakfast reading *Hemp Industry Daily* at the Tangerine restaurant in Boulder and the waiter would stop and tell me that he was in the Hemp Space too and knew a guy . . . They say every waitron in LA is an aspiring actor or screenwriter; every waitron in Colorado was an aspiring hemp broker.

So, I'd done the due diligence researching opportunities, worked the problem, and came up empty-handed. I couldn't believe there was no pasture that hadn't already been trampled and overgrazed in what was essentially the very first year of legal hemp. That's a testament, I suppose, to the entrepreneurial zeal of America. I've seen this before. You think you have an idea nobody's ever thought of and you want to start a business. You do a little research, and you find out that this is such a huge country and such a massive economy that your idea is not only not new, it's already an established industry, highly competitive, and there's even a trade show every year in Indianapolis.

Knowing all that, I still believed I was overlooking a key element somewhere. I just had to find it.

———

All around me, the boom was on. It wasn't just hemp, of course; the legalization of marijuana in Colorado a few years earlier had sprouted legions of pot pilgrims making the journey to Colorado to experience hassle-free cannabis usage. These folks, called narcotourists, added a nice sales boost to the legal marijuana dispensaries that were also popping up on every corner. The dispensaries, easily identified by sight because of the ubiquitous green cross and by nose because of that peculiar smell, also fostered an employment boost. Selling legal weed over the counter effectively is a skilled occupation and the practitioners call themselves "budtenders." Like DJs and bartenders, successful budtenders accumulate a following and are in high demand. Yes, there is a type. They are usually males in their late twenties. Facial hair and a man bun are assets. Ethnicity and skin color are irrelevant. What they all share is a smooth omniscient patter, like that of an NPR reporter or a well-trained butler. No mysteries, no judgment, just a wealth of expertise. They honed their skills telling war stories to one another, and the coffee shops of Boulder overflowed with ectomorphs in Oxford shirts regaling their rapt fellows with tales of rubes from Nebraska who didn't know their indica from their sativa.

The first time I encountered a budtender in the wild was in downtown Boulder with a relative of mine who was visiting

Colorado. He was a narcotourist—he'd come west to smoke legal weed without threat, and possibly to bring some home. All he could talk about when he got here was about visiting his first dispensary. He was panting to go first thing the next morning, which made me laugh. I told him we'd have time for a sleep-in, breakfast, and a five-mile hike before anybody would be turning on the Open sign at any dispensary in Colorado. Still, being a good Colorado host, I drove him to a dispensary downtown late that morning, and while we sat in the car waiting for the place to open, he started to get apprehensive.

"A Colorado dispensary! This is exciting. The thing is, I've never bought weed from anyone I didn't know. What happens when we go in?"

"I think we have to show some ID, so they know we're over twenty-one. I think they take a picture of it. I'm not sure. I've never been inside one of these either."

"ID? Like my driver's license?"

"Yeah. Like in a liquor store."

"What if the deep state is monitoring entrants to these places? Maybe they'll tell my boss and I'll get fired." My relative was a district manager for half a dozen Burger Kings.

"I think whatever deep state you're referring to might have other priorities. There are millions of people going into dispensaries. I think your job is safe. Your job is working eighty hours a week juggling scheduling nightmares, calling no-shows, monitoring petty theft, and ignoring at-work drug use. In return for that you get a salary of $45K and two weeks' vacation. I can't imagine people are lining up to replace you. I'm sure your bosses know that."

"That kind of hurts. I love my job. I just don't like my bosses."

"And I respect you the more for loving it. Join the club about the bosses. It's a big club. All I'm saying is that nobody's going to be monitoring your activity here. You probably have more cameras on you going into a 7–Eleven to buy a pack of Newports than you have here."

"Ok, if you say so. It's just new."

"Let's go. They've turned on the Open sign."

We went over to the door and there was a line. Really? A line? At 11 a.m. on a Tuesday morning? We didn't wait long and were greeted in the lobby by a tall, very polite young man who asked for our IDs and inquired, "Are you here for medicinal or recreational?"

This threw us both out of whatever stride we might have had. We looked at each other, confused. I decided to take the lead as the Colorado resident.

"We're not sure. What's the difference?"

"If you have a medical condition and a pink card, you go through door A. If you're participating in the cannabis revolution for recreational use, you go through door B."

My relative had recovered his bearings. "I want to smoke a bowl before skiing tomorrow. Maybe one today after lunch. Maybe another after dinner."

"Welcome. You're definitely door B."

That was easier than we thought. We were clicked through door B and entered a brightly lit room with a bunch of glass-fronted counters. On display were soup containers, chocolate bars, gummies, sandwiches, and some buds. It looked like a New York deli. The budtender, forty years younger than both of us, looked us over with an avuncular mien.

"Good morning, gentlemen! I'm Brandon, though my friends call me Koala. How can I help you today? Are you looking for indica or sativa?"

"Huh?"

"You're new here, I can see that. Welcome to Colorado. Indica has a more relaxing tone and sativa a more stimulating one. Within those parameters we've developed strains to fit various requirements. We have an indica here to reduce anxiety, another to develop relaxed concentration, another to just veg out. On the sativa side, we have a sports strain for better performance, another for resilience, and another for mental acuity. We have THC concentrations from 1% to 85%. We also have shatter, kush, wax, and vapes."

"What's with all the food?"

"Many of our clients prefer to ingest their cannabis via the alimentary system versus the pulmonary system. Some consider it a superior delivery method."

"Sure. Sounds fine. Look, I'm here visiting Colorado. I'm going skiing. I just want to cop a little buzz out on the hill. Burn a little piece of bud from my one-hitter between runs."

"I'll suggest our indica sativa 'Mixed Grill.' Want to test a bud?"

"You mean smoke some here?"

"Certainly not, sir. That would violate the wise proscriptions laid out by the state of Colorado for your protection. I was asking if you'd want to smell it."

"Sure."

Koala shimmered away and returned with a pair of forceps. He speared a bud and put it in front of the relative's nose.

"What do you think of the bouquet?"

"Better than the stuff I buy at home. How much?"

"Our pricing structure is fluid, sir. We generally sell by the gram. You appear to be a connoisseur from the twentieth-century cannabis vanguard. I mean that most respectfully. I'll suggest you're more familiar with the English units of measurement. For your reference point, there are 28.6 grams to an ounce."

"I'll take two grams of the barbecue."

"Mixed Grill, sir."

"Right. Sorry. How much of this should I burn at a time?"

"If it's your intention to burn the substance, I'd say, offhand, you can burn it at will. If you intend to inhale the residue however, I'd go slowly. As you are undoubtably aware, the inhalation of cannabis has almost immediate effects. You'd be best served by our offerings if you began with a modicum of restraint."

"This is heavy shit, huh?"

"I personally wouldn't characterize it that way, but I'd suggest a walk before the marathon. Perhaps more appropriately, the glide before the ski. You'd not want to spend your holiday in the lodge ordering innumerable plates of loaded nachos when the snow conditions are reportedly so agreeable."

"Got it. I don't want to be sidelined with the munchies. Hey thanks, Koala."

———

In late August, the weedwhackers asked me to a meeting at a coffee shop in Boulder. I'd been working with them off and on since I'd furnished them with a cashflow chart and started watering seedlings a few months before. My projection had them spending well over $400,000 to get them from seed to sale, which would have taken any hemp farmer by surprise. Overlooking facts in favor of ambition is a classic small business mistake, and one I've made over and over. Sitting at the café with the weedwhackers, I sipped my coffee and listened to the budtenders all around us swap war stories. It was an enjoyable scene.

After a while, Larry, the lead weedwhacker, started it off.

"We're going to be harvesting mid- to late September. Between irrigation and fertilizer issues, weeding, mowing, cross-pollination problems, and the creeping THC content of the crop, we haven't yet figured out our post-harvest plan."

This made them exactly like everyone else. Larry then laid out the steps necessary to turn the plants into smokeable hemp flower.

"First, we need to hang-dry the plants. For that we'll need three vinyl-covered metal hoophouses. I'm not talking about some backyard thing. I'm talking about three warehouses you can drive a tractor-trailer into. We have room on the farm to place them, but we don't have the money to buy them or the contractors to build them. Then we'll need to figure out a way to hang the plants, plus find a bunch of laborers to do the work. They need to be built and plant-ready in the next three weeks. After drying, we'll need at least one bucking machine, probably two, at least one trimming machine, a few dozen fans and humidifiers to control the rate of drying, and heavy-duty generators to power it all. You've been with us from the start and did that financial thing from before, so we figured we'd tell you our challenges. Maybe you can come up with an idea or a solution?"

"What *do* you have?" I asked.

"Well, there's all my experience."

"Have you actually done a large project like this before?"

"Not actually, no. But I know how it's supposed to be done."

"That's good because I definitely don't know how it's supposed to be done. Sounds like you guys have a thorny business problem. Let me think about this and we can meet again in a couple of days."

"Sure, a couple of days is fine, but think fast, the clock is running."

This was interesting. Post-harvest processing to turn the crop into smokeable hemp flower. *Hmmm.* I'd read nothing about this in all my research, and nobody had spoken about it even though it was the elephant in the room.

Colorado had 2,554 growers putting up over 80,000 acres of hemp. Granted, lots of that was going to biomass, which had its own infrastructure, sort of, but smokeable flower required hang-drying, bucking, and trimming, and I knew *all* of the small growers in Colorado were growing for smokeable flower. Who was going to do all that work? The weedwhackers posed that question to me three weeks before harvest and had no answer. A fair proportion of the other 2,553 growers would be asking it soon enough. They wouldn't have an answer either.

There were about a hundred hemp registrations in Boulder County and the average hemp farm was about six acres, so most of these folks were small. I was fairly sure few of them would have hoophouses, barns, or warehouses to dry their hemp. I was absolutely sure none of them would have the machinery to buck and trim their crop into smokeable hemp flower. I'd spent a year researching hemp before buying my farm, and the five months since April, other than working at various farms, immersing myself in the intricacies of hemp processing and sales. Trying to separate fact from fiction was an annoying yet illuminating exercise. I'd run down a lot of promising leads that turned into dead ends, but there was one nugget of gold hiding at the bottom:

Almost nobody had a post-harvest plan to turn their plants into smokeable flower.

The weedwhackers were smarter than the average grower, but they weren't any further along in figuring out what to do with tons of giant plants than anyone else. It was hard to believe, but all the growers were task-saturated just bringing their crop to harvest and hadn't laid out a plan ahead of time for the post-harvest steps.

Maybe they thought they'd have time to figure that part out, or maybe they thought demand would be so strong that someone would ride up on a horse and save the day.

I had been wondering if I was ever going to find a place in the Hemp Space. I had almost despaired of finding a niche, though I knew that in a brand-new industry there had to be inefficiencies and opportunities. Since I couldn't find any, I'd begun to doubt my business acumen. I also had a fear of missing out on this exciting first year of legal hemp, and, on a more practical side, I had to pay for a thirty-six-acre farm that I wasn't farming. That was when the weedwhackers came to me with their problem and I hatched my business plan, if you can call it that. I decided I'd do the post-harvest processing for the weedwhackers and tack on as many other growers as space and time allowed. I'd buy and build the hoophouses, dry the plants, purchase the required machinery, get the labor, and deliver sellable smokeable flower back to the grower. This was within my skillset and investment limit.

I had stumbled onto the emerging market inefficiency that I'd known intuitively was there but hadn't been able to find. Once I found it, "post-harvest processing" became poetry set to music. I saw it all at once in a flash of inspiration: in a little over a month, there'd be legions of desperate growers looking to process their hemp into flower. Those same growers who couldn't find time to talk to me before would be lining up because I'd be the only guy around who could turn their crop into a product.

Demand was still racing ahead. I'd have to move very fast. The weedwhackers needed three massive hoophouses built, because there were no buildings available anywhere on the Front Range to hang dry hemp plants. Available warehouse space just didn't exist. I'd seen this up close, coming from the trucking world. Regular transport and storage companies couldn't find space either. So many buildings were being leased to weed growers, hemp extractors, and processors at premium rates that they were squeezing the old economy out, except for Amazon, which was hoovering up warehouse space even faster than the hemp and cannabis boys. Companies like ProLogis, the largest industrial real estate company in the world, with a billion square feet of warehousing in its maw, was building warehouse space in Denver at a feverish rate. Over the past two years, 12 million square feet of warehouse space had been built in the Denver metro area, and demand was still racing ahead of supply.

I spent the next couple of days in a frenzy of financial projections trying to get a handle on what it would cost and what I could charge for the service. There was little to go on. Capital costs were relatively easy to figure out. The hoophouses were $10,000 each, but what it might cost to erect them, fortify them, and install ten miles of rope to hang the plants was a mystery. I knew I'd need at least $150,000 worth of bucking and trimming machines, fans, generators, tools, and humidifiers. I'd need to find and hire an army of workers. I'd need clippers, gloves, dumpsters, and trash removal. How much time and labor it might cost to turn those plants into buds I'd have to figure out. Nobody who'd done it before was talking, and frankly, there weren't many folks who had done it on the scale I was planning. Maybe in Oregon there were, but not in Colorado, and Oregon hempsters were legendary for their sealed lips.

This isn't how I'd set up my previous businesses. In the past I'd been inside an industry, usually for a good long while, before making a move. I got acquainted with the players, the marketplace, and discovered a niche that I researched, and then I developed a short-, medium-, and long-term plan to enter the market and build up customers, trust, and momentum. It was a careful, patient, slow process, with the real payoff slated to come years later. Nobody I ever met in the Hemp Space was doing that. It was all do-it-now or get left behind, mostly by folks who'd never run so much as a shoeshine stand. Rather than scaring me, that made me confident. If bumps in the road came, I was sure I could navigate them better than a basement weed grower turned farmer, or an ex-banker turned CBD salesman.

I met again with the weedwhackers a few days later and told them I'd take on their post-harvest processing completely. I'd finance the entire operation, put their crop first, and then process for other farmers as time and space allowed. Since there were no cost metrics, we agreed to defer any pricing for the services performed until after the final costs were tabulated and we'd meet to determine fair compensation. We were all thrilled. It was perfect: for them, there would be no money upfront for post-harvesting, first place in line, three giant hoophouses to be built on their farm, and they'd oversee the process since I had no clue how to process hemp. For me, I'd earn a reasonable return for services rendered. We'd all be rich and happy. We agreed then and there on handshakes to go forward, and the room was awash with good fellowship and excitement.

PART II
RUNNING DOWN A DREAM

Chapter 5
HOOPHOUSES

Entrepreneurship is a word I generally avoid because it's too long and self-aggrandizing for my delicate sensibilities. What I cherish is the exchange of goods and services to mutual benefit that owning a business creates. A hallmark of civilization is our capacity to trade fairly with one another. That practice has saved *Homo sapiens* from bigger, faster, and better-toothed predators since the beginning of time. It can be a hot dog stand (which I operated one summer) or an international textile trading firm (which I operated for over a decade); whatever the business is, it deserves respect and so does the person who started it. That's the story I tell myself when I'm elevated with lofty sentiments. A different story might be that I ended up working for myself because I was an unskilled Eastern preppie and opinionated know-it-all whom no business owner would ever consider hiring. One of the nice things about getting older is that whatever the real story is or was, it doesn't matter anymore.

What mattered now was that all my cylinders were firing when I walked the weedwhacker farm alone, staking out the hoophouses. My heart was light, and my spirits were soaring. Another enterprise!

Maybe a business vision eventually turns into Apple, or maybe not, but they all start with a dreamer walking alone with nothing but an idea. It's a beautiful thing never to be truly understood except by those who have trodden that solitary path. If your enterprise doesn't turn into billions, you can often turn it into something successful enough to support your family and your employees. That's pretty great.

What's not often discussed in this great American myth of startups is that one-fifth of them fail in their first year and over half fail before five years. After ten years, not even a third are left standing. Those dismal numbers wouldn't work at all for a surgeon or a dry cleaner, but the statistics never seem to stop anyone from following their dream. I know why, too. It's because it's exciting for the person starting up, and the entire culture encourages the dream though not, alas, the reality. Win or lose, the business owner will carry the experience of that startup forever. If the business fails, the operator will have a deeper understanding of many things, and failure can also have surprising downstream benefits that lead to later success.

I wasn't looking at the odds in this venture any more than I'd looked at them with any other startup I'd done. I was looking at the upside. My expectations were different, too. This wasn't going to be a build-up of trust and market share with income increasing over time. This was a boom, and I knew it. I'd need to make my money quickly and get out before the music stopped and the last chair was taken. I was sure I could navigate that better than the starry-eyed hemp clerics. I didn't actually *know* that, but I figured the probabilities were in my favor as a business veteran. One thing I did know was that if prices held firm, a ten-acre hemp farm would yield about 5,000 pounds of smokeable flower, and with the residual biomass would gross almost two million bucks. Even if my processing fee was a quarter of that, my clients would be happy since their crop would be worthless without my services.

While all this was happening quickly, it was really a culmination of well over a year's preparation in the Hemp Space. It's true that I had gone ahead and bought a farm, but I'd been careful since then. I didn't get caught in the various webs of extraction, consumer branding, or any of the other Hemp Space box canyons. What the weedwhackers needed was a careful businessman. That's someone who doesn't overlook facts and keeps his head out of the sand. That's someone who can build a cashflow projection and understand financial statements. That's someone who can build a business from disparate and unreliable information, someone who can act fast and use his own capital. In short, someone like me. Even though I say it myself, people with those skills and capital usually aren't available on short notice, to perform such a complicated task, in a recently illegal industry, with a trio of amateur hemp farmers as your resident expertise.

———

As the field marshal of this new enterprise, the first thing I'd need would be a general who'd manage all this on the ground. I immediately thought of my nephew, Pierce, who lived in Denver. He was a thirty-five-year-old sales executive who had told me more than once that he was tired of his job. He was six feet four inches of millennial smarts and might be trolling for a new opportunity. I called him up and gave him my pitch.

"Here's the deal, Pierce. You'll have to take a pay cut, work seven very long days a week, and be on a steep learning curve first as a construction manager, then as a hemp processor. After that, you're probably going to be selling this stuff, and after that—"

"I'm in."

"That's it? You're in?"

"I'm in. I've hit the ceiling here at my job and all the chatter in Denver these days is about hemp and CBD. There might be a solid upside here. It's time for a change, anyway. I want to be outside, doing different stuff every day. I'm in a rut."

"You'll certainly be outside doing different stuff every day. I'm not sure how this is going to play out, though. It's not a sure thing." Actually, in my mind it *was* a sure thing, but I wanted to be careful with my nephew.

"I already told you, I'm in. Are you trying to talk me out of it?"

"Not at all, but I've lived my whole life this way. I'm very comfortable with my face in the wind running small businesses. That risk profile doesn't suit everyone. I don't take on the responsibility of an employee lightly either, especially in a startup where frankly I've no idea of what's really going on. This is moving faster than I'm used to and that's new for me too. You already have a good job. This whole thing could flame out. I'm fine if I get burned but I don't want your career to be collateral damage . . . unless you're mentally prepared for it."

"I'm mentally prepared to kick some ass, take some names, and make some real money. If it doesn't work out, I'm mentally prepared to sell pencils on the Sixteenth Street Mall if I have to. I've had my face in the wind before this too, you know."

"OK then. Let's do it."

Pierce was not only my nephew; I was godfather at his christening and had watched him grow up and attended his graduation from Tulane. We'd always got on well, but then Pierce got on well with everyone. He's a big man. Big body, big personality, big brain, and big witty mouth, full of a fun, gregarious patter intended to put you at your ease.

After some unproductive post-college years, he'd been living in Denver and making his way. Since I was divorced and living in Boulder and my nearest relation was in St. Louis, we kept close. Pierce's dad, who happened to be my best friend, died at sixty-two of melanoma. That brought us closer.

Pierce was engaged to be married and was eager to make some real money. He liked Denver and he'd also seen the house prices in the area. The opening price point was $450,000, and for that he'd not get what he and his fiancée wanted but have to settle for some cookie-cutter ranch house in a treeless subdivision so far east of Denver they might as well be in Kansas. (As a retired mover, I've seen the inside of thousands of homes and navigated subdivisions from Key West to Vancouver. It's made me a horrible snob—a trait shared by virtually all movers. I remember my regular helper, Carlos Ruiz, who resided with his extensive progeny in a leaky Winnebago on a residential trailer park plot just below the unfashionable eastern fringe of Firestone, Colorado. Carlos, who got his own furniture from Goodwill, or Aaron's when he felt flush, complained constantly about the low-quality furniture he was being paid to move. "I'm sick of moving fiberboard dressers into basements with oversized window wells. Dug out basements are the big thing. You know why? Because they're beautiful? No, because it's a cheap way to add living space. It's underground! Rats live underground. Where are the Duncan Fyfe highboys anymore? And these houses! Plastic shit. If they caught fire, you'd die of poison air before the smoke alarm even had a chance to scream." Carlos didn't have a bank account, but his aesthetic sense was offended. He felt he was wasting his excellent moving skills bringing Walmart nightstands into tract houses. Houses he couldn't afford in seven lifetimes, but so what? He's a true-blue mover snob, God bless him, and so am I.)

Pierce and his soon-to-be-wife were ready to start a family and, being in their mid-thirties, knew the clock was running. He wanted to make six figures and wanted it soon. They didn't need the house of their dreams, but they did need a real roof and a real income, so a foray into the booming Hemp Space looked attractive to them too.

I also wanted to work with my godson and make some money with him. I knew it was a risky proposition, but I was figuring that at my age this might be my last chance to make a big score. I was not lending a helping hand to a relative or doing him any kind of favor; I was upending his stable world and bringing him into the alternate universe of small business management. This was a world I knew well, and loved, but it's definitely not for folks who worry every day about things like mortgage payments. Still, guys like me are always on the lookout for smart people with a work ethic, skills, and ambition. Pierce had all those and together I knew we'd have a strong team.

My first task when starting a new business has always been to draft an organizational chart. An org chart details all the tasks a business requires and who's going to do them. It's a slog until you get used to it, but entirely necessary. Even a hot dog stand needs an org chart.

Pierce and I needed to get the three hoophouses built in two weeks and then equip them in time for harvest. I'm good at this type of thing, being very focused and organized. I learned work-flow from my second business in the 1980s as an owner–operator contracted to a van line. We didn't call the moving industry the Moving Space and we didn't imbue the work with much glamor or revolutionary vision for a brave new world. We needed to empty houses in the shortest amount of time and load a truck in an organized manner without destroying people's stuff. It was an ideal environment for a young man to learn efficiency, independent decision-making, aggressive problem-solving, and managing an unruly workforce.

I had my general. All I needed now for staff was an officer or two, and a lot of infantry.

I'm a decent businessman, but I have gaps. One of those is a dearth of wild imagination when it comes to naming my enterprises. A company called Häagen-Dazs or Google or Adidas wouldn't have made it off my desk, while the Container Store or Home Goods would have made me giddy with delight. True to my roots, I decided to call this new enterprise Front Range Hemp Harvesting Services, LLC. A mouthful certainly, possibly a tad grandiose, but direct and clear.

Once I'd made my org chart, I went over to the weedwhacker farm to figure out where the hoophouses would go. This is one of those sweet spots when starting a business. You're there at the very beginning when you have the optimism, the vision, and the view of a clear empty field, and, well, almost every new business has a humble start. My third business, importing sweaters from Ireland, started in a back-alley basement in a run-down strip mall in Stamford, Connecticut. It was certainly humble, but it was *mine*. That enterprise eventually morphed into a multi-million-dollar business with offices in a Manhattan skyscraper and headquarters on Nantucket Island. I used to charter airplanes to the New York office fairly regularly to snap wet towels at the asses of my sales team. After a nice lunch at the garmento-infused Arno restaurant on Thirty-Eighth Street, I'd fly home in time for a 3 p.m. County Commission meeting.

Whatever satisfaction I may have gotten from landing at Teterboro and walking ten steps to the waiting limo was not nearly as energizing as turning the key for the first time on that basement alley door in Stamford. I've never felt more alive, vibrant, and important than I was in those first moments of my real brick-and-mortar enterprise. I was doing my calculations and focusing my vision. It belonged only to me and was a defining moment that carries a poignancy and thrill that's never been matched.

Avoiding bull snakes and rusting farm detritus, I figured out the hoophouse locations with a hundred-foot tape measure and pounded in surveyor stakes. There were eagles overhead and horses in the paddock as I did my sums. This bucolic place was about to fundamentally change, and that's what's odd about farming. My cultural view of farming came from John Deere commercials, which typically starred a slim white man from a place like Iowa with dirt in his fingernails sampling soil or looking toward the lovely sunset with his wife and baby fawning over his acreage and manly mien. Very nice and not entirely fictional—the true part being that farming is really all about machinery. Sure, you get to work outside—usually underneath a machine, often in mud, banging a malfunctioning implement with a hammer or wrench to make it behave like it did in the commercial.

I had ordered the three monster hoophouses on August 26 and they were scheduled for delivery September 9. Each one, when assembled, would be 15 feet tall, 30 feet wide, and 100 feet long. The salesman at the manufacturer was a breezy New Englander with a patter of platitudes designed to put nervous customers like me at ease about assembling his product. The longer I've been in Colorado, the more I've found that East Coast attitude annoying, though it hasn't been completely sanded off me yet either. (There will always be some Western things I can't pull off no matter how long I'm out here. For example, I can't wear a cowboy hat. I'm always trying them on at Murdoch's, my local farm and ranch store. They have an entire wall of hats, another wall of boots, and 5,000 square feet of Carhartt work clothes. Out back, the yard is strewn with gates, barbed wire, cattle guards, and feed troughs. I love the place. Every time I'm there I try on maybe a dozen different hats and check myself in the mirror. The salesperson's face always falls whenever I put one on. No matter what shape lands on my head I always look like a guy from Connecticut trying to wear a cowboy hat.)

I'd checked out the hoophouse assembly instructions online and wasn't sanguine about our abilities. A large hoophouse has about 5,000 parts. After all my years as a mover, I was more than familiar with the challenges of assembling things like IKEA furniture. Anyone who's worked with me has heard me grumble more than once about those Swedish psychopaths and their propensity for accidentally leaving out a key piece of information on the instructions or neglecting to include the custom cam bolts illustrated in Figure 5A.

We had three of these hoophouses to assemble, equip, and reinforce in a roughly two-week window, since the weedwhackers' plants were at risk of turning into hot hemp and becoming worthless.

Luckily, the three tractor-trailers arrived on schedule, and I assisted the drivers in dumping their loads with a tractor that was on the farm. My experience from the moving industry proved vital, because I remembered Manuel, a helper of mine on moving jobs from time to time over the past decade.

Manuel is a man of rare intelligence who has nevertheless had no permanent employment in the ten years I've known him. He's a carpenter, an electrician, a plumber, a concrete man, a roofer, a welder, and a drywaller. Someone once carved up his face with a broken wine bottle and he has a scar that runs from his ear and down his neck. He doesn't know how he lived through that one. I can only assume that his private life is complicated, but he's never displayed that in his working life with me. He's always been calm and professional, with an easygoing competence no matter what's tossed at him. He takes his pay in cash, naturally.

Manuel's employment issues are a conundrum I've often thought about and the only thing I can come up with is respect. I've always treated Manuel that way and it's not difficult because I do respect him; he's a dedicated, assiduous, and reliable worker. Still, in Longmont, Colorado, where the population is about 50% Latino, plenty of Anglos lump all these brown folks together into an amorphous mass of awkward foreigners. The irony is that Manuel, even though he speaks with a tiny lilting Spanish accent, is a native-born American and a graduate of Longmont High School. He's a hell of a lot smarter than I am, and he knows it, but he's often treated poorly, and I think that pisses him off. If he doesn't get the respect he thinks he deserves, well then, fuck off gringo. He wouldn't say that, though; he'd just disappear.

I've seen this many times on moving trucks over the decades. Faced with gringo power—over employment or anything else— some folks will just nod, say yes, and vaporize. Naturally, this drives Anglos batshit, but it's perfectly reasonable behavior. In fact, it's kind of sweet and gentle, and a way to get by without being obnoxious. I like it, except when I'm depending upon my main guy Francisco to meet me in Colorado Springs for moving work and he's a no-show. I'll find out later that Francisco hates the Springs and, having been hassled there one too many times, he just won't go.

I've pretty much figured it out now: you can tell from lack of eye contact and some foot shuffling that when a certain guy says yes, he means, well, precisely, no. After all the angst about the supposed deception has burned up, you realize it's just one of those cultural differences that can be enriching and, frankly, illuminating. Maybe it's better not to be confrontational. If you can read the body language, or take the time to figure it out, or get out of your own gringo skin for five seconds, you'll realize he's actually, in his way, being truthful. It took me a long time working with guys like Francisco and Manuel just to notice their verbal and physical cues, and even longer to translate them.

All that said, when the chips are down and you're looking for the Guy, Manuel is that guy. He's soft-hearted too, and like many of the down-and-out non-whites I've worked with, he wants to help out if he can. So I called him up, told him I was in a bind, and, as always trying to be as direct and honest as possible, explained that it was a tough job requiring his particular skills. He knew I was buttering him up, not that that bothered him. Compliments, genuine or not, were rare and therefore welcome. He was receptive, in his reticent way. I asked him what he'd been up to employment-wise.

"This and that," he said. "Nothing special." Translation: *Zero.*

"I've got a month minimum. Construction job. Twenty bucks an hour. How does that sound?"

"I'll have to check my schedule. How about twenty-five an hour? Do you need anyone else?" Translation: *Yes, but I'm not saying yes right now or it will look like I'm desperate. I know you'll pay me more than $20. Will you hire my pals or relatives who are also between jobs?*

"I need every hand on deck you can muster."

There was a pause—and I realized that my Eastern analogy of mustering hands on a ship might be mystifying to someone of his background in landlocked Colorado. I've run into this problem my whole life. For some reason, I refuse to take my diction down. It happened all the time in truck stops too. People thought I was being superior, but I thought it was just the opposite. I thought it would be patronizing to adjust to somebody's language level. Most people are pretty smart and a regional accent is no indicator of intelligence. I have the same issue with children. I don't talk down to them, I don't change my voice level, I don't simplify my vocabulary. I don't ask dumb questions that grownups ask, like "What grade are you in now?" That this behavior is mostly unsuccessful somehow never changes my tactics. In Manuel's case here, I simply ignored it and forged ahead.

"Call Francisco and Jake and Bobby. I need all the good guys we both know."

"What is it?" Translation: *Is this an opportunity I want to share with folks close to me?*

"I knew you'd get around to that. We're building greenhouses. Big ones. Ought to be interesting."

"Twenty-five bucks an hour cash is interesting. Work is work. I'll get back to you." Translation: *$25 an hour has now become the agreed wage. It's cash, meaning, off the books. I'll do it, but I'm not going to show any enthusiasm.*

"When?"

"Mañana." Translation: *Not today.*

"How about tomorrow? I need to know."

"Mañana means tomorrow, gringo." Translation: *I'm bilingual, you're not.*

"Manuel, we have history together. I know about four words in Spanish and one of them is mañana and we both know it doesn't mean tomorrow, it means not today. I'm sure you appreciate the nuance. If you don't, I do. So how about you call me tomorrow."

"OK," he said. Translation: *Don't count on it.*

I was reasonably confident he'd call back, though not necessarily the next day. Any display of desperation, or even eagerness, was not in the script, which is what this whole quasi-negotiation was. No matter their normally straitened circumstances, I had to acknowledge that these guys would be doing me a favor by working under the table for twenty-five bucks an hour, which is damn good money by any measure, especially when it was going to be a month or two of twelve- to fourteen-hour days.

Paying in cash is another thing that's attractive to folks in this particular American economic netherworld. Taxes, Social Security numbers, 1099s, and W2s are not considered assets or investments in this milieu. They are viewed as a predictable slope ending inevitably into contact with government, and government contact has rarely turned out well for any of these folks, their experience being mainly to do with traffic stops or ICE visits, and those *never* end to their advantage.

While some of this might sound like there's labor conflict, it's more a subtle and constant pressure to get paid more than I'm offering and to maintain dignity. If I paid Manuel fifty an hour, he'd be angling for fifty-five. It's a reflex, not an argument. Francisco once came to me on a job like this and showed me the labor rules he'd found on his phone. It said he was supposed to get fifteen-minute breaks every four hours, and time and a half after forty hours of work. I countered by showing him the tax table of withholding wages and said if he wanted to go legit, he'd get his breaks and overtime and lose about a third of his pay to Uncle Sam. I never heard a word after that about labor laws.

The nice part of all this is that guys like Francisco and Manuel know how to work and know how I like to work, which is all day long without stopping except for a short lunch. The bottom line is that we all *like* to work hard and work smart with other folks who do it that way. That's not typical in most work environments. It takes time, a little conflict, and then mutual forgiveness, to achieve.

Manuel called the next morning and said he could start anytime and would bring Jake and his cousin Stevie. (Francisco was unavailable, which could mean anything: jail, part-time work, football season, or just not feeling it.) I was thrilled. Jake had been another one of my main men when I was working as a mover. He was a bull of a worker also living through a couple decades of bad luck.

"Jake's coming?"

"Sure." Translation: *He's got nothing else going on workwise.*

"Great. How's he been?"

"Ah you know. He's living in a trailer with his family on some-body's ranch but he's ready for another crib. Got any room on that farm for Jake's camper?" Translation: *Jake needs to move.*

This was perfect for me. I'd have my twenty-four-hour security service.

"I think that would be OK. I'll have to check with the owner, though."

"Jake can bring his camper over today, if that works." Transla-tion: *Jake needs to move now.*

"I'll let you know about Jake's camper, Manuel."

"When?" Translation: *This is a crisis for Jake.*

"Mañana," I said, falling easily into the pattern.

The weedwhackers had been concerned about security from the start, and one of them knew Jake because Jake had moved him several times. I'm not saying this weedwhacker's relocations might have had anything to do with marijuana growing, but folks growing indoor weed often find themselves switching homes on short notice when their landlord figures out the smell from the basement. One whiff, one short conversation, and some-body's calling Jake to book the U-Haul. You can be sure these summary evictions won't require any sheriff's deputy nailing a notice on the door.

Having Jake living in his camper on-site was just fine with the weedwhackers and fine with me too. I explained all this to Jake; not only was he going to have a couple months' work at the site, for himself, his wife, and his sons, but he had a secure place to put his camper, and he would be the security detail. Jake liked the sound of all that. When he asked what his pay for security was going to be. I told him we'd buy him a generator, pay for the gas, and he'd pay no rent for the camper spot. He didn't like that, but seeing as he had overstayed his welcome where he was and had nowhere else to go, he accepted his new position.

Things were falling neatly into place. Pierce had connections with the Salvation Army rehab center in Denver that found employment for their graduates, and we added two more to the crew. The Salvation Army guys were thoughtful and entertaining colleagues. The program they were in was strict, requiring an eighteen-month residential commitment in the facility. There was no fee for the program, but one infraction and boom, it was back onto the streets or back into prison. Both these guys had completed the program and were on work release. I've spent a fair amount of time with addicts and petty criminals because many of the laborers I hired as movers came from the same vortex. I've always been impressed by their frankness and intelligence. Their status at the bottom of the American Dream shouldn't be held against them, and the guys Pierce hired were no exceptions. I'm not sure putting them into work processing hemp was the best environment for them but I had my own problems, like getting hoophouses built, and they were happy to get the work.

Such were the modest beginnings of Front Range Hemp Harvesting Services, LLC. Three oft-mistreated Latinos with spotty work histories, three Salvation Army grads, and one very stressed-out but extremely optimistic former truck driver. The magnificent seven.

We started at the weedwhacker farm one lovely September morning at 8 a.m. Pierce had picked up the two Denver guys at the halfway house and Manuel's crew was already there. We went through the couple dozen pallets full of hoophouse parts, shipped in no discernible order, and tried to make sense of what we had. I'd given Manuel a binder with the assembly instructions a couple of days earlier for him to review, and Pierce had his own binder. I can't say we covered ourselves in glory that first day. Pierce spent most of the morning on the phone with the manufacturer's customer service person trying to figure out what was what, while Manuel quietly picked his way through the pallets making notes on a little pad. We broke for lunch having done nothing beyond reestablishing the four corners for each hoophouse, shoveling horseshit, and moving scrap metal from the site. After lunch Pierce and Manuel had a little huddle and Manuel came up to me and said:

"I might have figured a few things out. Would you mind going to Home Depot and getting some stuff?" He handed me a list.

"Some stuff" consisted of six Ryobi power drills with extra chargers and batteries, dozens of socket bits, a gas-powered auger to make holes in the ground, a gas-powered hammer to drill the posts, three 9,000-watt generators, 10,000 feet of rope, four 12-foot construction ladders, one hundred 16-foot 2x4s, eighteen 16-foot 4x4s, one hundred 2x6s, twelve bags of cement, three shovels, four sledgehammers, a 100-foot tape measure, four 8-foot stackable scaffolds, twelve trash barrels, and a 10-gallon water container.

I looked over the list in shock. All I could say was, "I already have a 100-foot tape measure."

"Then cross it off."

"Water container?"

"I didn't see a tap anywhere. Are you gonna buy water bottles over at the convenience store for the next three months?"

As always, Manuel was both polite and correct.

I returned a few hours later having spent $35,000.

Manuel then suggested I rent a couple 40-foot storage containers and two 40-foot dumpsters. Finally, he mentioned that a chainsaw and a porta-potty might come in handy. Manuel had foreseen the eventual scale of this enterprise. I hadn't.

So it began. It was thirty grand for the hoophouses, so I was in for $65,000 already and all we had was a pile of pallets sitting on the ground surrounded by horseshit and seven guys standing around costing $175 an hour in aggregate, or three bucks a minute, give or take. I'd get used to this eventually, but I wasn't used to it yet. All the money to finance this piece of madness or inspiration, depending upon how it all ended up, was coming out of my retirement account.

Hoophouses consist of a series of hollow steel pipes that fit together into a large hoop. There are two six-foot pipes that get driven four feet into the ground, so two feet are sticking up. Then two four-foot pipes that go straight up and four angled pipes that meet in the middle, fifteen feet aboveground, to form a truss. These are spaced four feet apart, so there are twenty-five sections in a 100-foot hoop house. Manuel sent the crew searching through the pallets to find and separate pipe sizes, putting them in marked piles while he was busy with his notebook, the 100-foot tape measure, and a can of fluorescent spray paint. I could see him moving down the field, occasionally scratching his head, and occasionally dropping a glob of blaze orange paint onto the ground.

A little while later he called the crew together and asked them if they wouldn't mind drilling a pipe at each paint dab. Pierce assigned the rehab boys to this and that's all they did for the next week or so. They'd attach a two-sided level to the pipe, one guy would hold the pipe level, and the other would fit the pneumatic hammer to the top of the pipe and hit the switch. The hammer made a loud *tut tut tut tut* sound as it banged the pipe into the ground. Jake and Stevie would follow and fit the first four-foot pipe into the one sticking out of the ground and secure it with Tek screws. Tek screws are self-tapping fasteners that drill into metal, eliminating the need to drill a pilot hole. Self-tapping is a highly relative term, since it still takes a lot of force to get the screw to bite into the metal. Now I understood Manuel's need for all the Ryobi power drills with the extra chargers and batteries. Each truss required forty Tek screws, with one guy to hold the fitting while the other guy held the drill, going higher and higher and finishing the drilling on scaffolds.

When this first part of the frame was up, the next step was to level the first truss, tie it off to the ground, make sure the spacing at the top was the same as at the bottom, and attach the ridge pole to lock each truss in position. Each hoophouse had two purlins halfway up to further lock in the trusses. Each purlin plus the ridge beam required tek screws to attach to each truss, so that was another three hundred drillings, mostly high up on a ladder. Along the sides at two feet up and six feet up we attached the 2x6s with bolts (more drilling) to secure the whole building. Second to last was attaching metal groove strips to the trusses, which the vinyl cover would fit onto. Another few hundred Tek screws and more labor. Finally, we put H-shaped anchors at each end, which were made of 20-foot-long 4x4s drilled four feet into the ground, cemented into place, and crossed by a single 30-foot wooden beam.

This, we hoped, would prevent the whole building from being swept away in a Colorado windstorm.

It took a week to construct our first hoophouse skeleton. Thanks to Manuel, Pierce, and the crew, it looked perfect. If this was a regular hoophouse it would be ready for the vinyl cover, but it wasn't. First, we had to level the ground inside and lay down a 30-by-100-foot heavy-duty tarp ($500), nailing it to the ground at intervals with long spikes and wide washers. Wall-to-wall carpeting.

We were planning on hanging seven and a half tons of wet hemp plants from the ceiling of each hoophouse, a use definitely not covered in the manufacturer's warranty. I had no idea whether the building would hold the weight, but Manuel had figured that out. A column every other truss, he said, should do the trick. The crew grabbed the 2x4s, cut them to size, notched the tops, and installed columns all the way down. We completed Hoophouse 1 at dusk on day eight and were enormously proud of our building. It wasn't quite finished, but we knew it would work.

There were several tasks pending. There were always tasks pending, and that's a big part of the attraction of business management. You get to perform triage every day. One task was attaching and electrifying the giant four-foot fans at one end and the louvered vents at the other. Manuel put away his carpenter's tool bag, which weighed about 80 pounds, pulled out his electrician's tool bag, and did the necromancy of applying power to the fans. Other tasks were attaching the roll-up doors, putting on the vinyl cover, and tying the ropes to hang the plants.

The vinyl cover had been making us all nervous. We'd watched videos of how this was done and how easily it could go wrong. The cover came in a five-foot-wide roll, but when opened would be 50 feet wide and 120 feet long. Even a tiny breath of wind was liable to take the whole thing into Nebraska. We decided to wait until dawn Sunday morning, when there'd be minimal wind, to put the cover on. Ten guys arrived at sun-up and we put a steel bar through the roll, built a little stand for the roll to sit on, and tied the end of the roll with a long rope. Then, pulling on the rope, we lifted the vinyl up over the first truss and snaked it along the ridge pole to the other end. It was only five feet wide at this point, because it would be unfolded down the sides. After securing each end tightly at the ridge, we unfolded it, and it fell soundlessly like a graceful birdcage cover to the ground, perfectly even on both sides. The crew then pulled one side tight and anchored the vinyl. That done, we went to the other side, pulled it tight, and anchored that. Hot damn! It looked like a giant greenhouse assembled by pros.

Our last job to get the hoophouse ready for plants was to position the ropes the plants would hang on. One of our new guys, who had deep experience in hemp processing, told us that the usual practice was to use ⅛-inch parachute cord to tie the ropes to the trusses. We adopted that plan, and the ropes were hung from the ceiling at two-foot intervals to make a row all the way down to the end. Then another set was tied two feet from that row, and so on until we reached the other side. Each row was 100 feet long, and the two-foot spacing on a 30-foot wide hoophouse meant we'd have fifteen rows of ropes going sideways and fifty rows going longways. Before we could hang them, though, we had to tie loop knots at two-foot intervals in each rope to hold the plants—that's 13,500 knots, and there's no such thing as pre-knotted rope, so they all had to be hand-tied. Each rope segment that started out at 25 feet ended up at 12 feet when all the knots were tied. Manuel did that simple calculation and asked me if I'd mind getting 56,250 feet of rope. That's more than ten miles.

I went all over the Front Range buying rolls of parachute cord at every Lowe's and Home Depot I could find. We'd been adding workers day by day and, while it wasn't yet an army, it was no longer the magnificent seven. There were about twenty people working, most of them tying knots eight hours a day.

By the time Hoophouse 1 was ready for plants, we'd been working for seventeen days. That timing was OK but not ideal, because the weedwhackers were suddenly ready to harvest and we still had Hoophouses 2 and 3 to build. The CBD/THC tests were showing that their hemp was getting hot rapidly, and they pushed the harvest date earlier. We got more workers, set up two shifts, and split the crews so we could start on the plants that were ready for harvesting.

———

Through all this work, Pierce was multitasking with fervor and competence. He'd show up around dawn and leave when it was dark. He had an intuitive skill of handling people effectively that I watched increase with every day on the job. Pierce could simultaneously let folks know he understood their problems while challenging them to measure up. This wasn't any kind of false front. Pierce had had his own failures and never forgot them when dealing with his staff. He was a natural in this chaotic environment, and he and Manuel were synchronized since they both knew workspaces and both spoke Spanish.

Manuel had become a different person. While always diffident and inordinately polite, Manuel had started to joke around with the crew. He was coming out of his shell and he and Pierce would jabber away in Iberian whispers throughout the day.

With those two at the helm, I shed my proclivity for micromanagement and spent my days at the building site filling generators with gas, filling the water dispenser, moving the tractor around for the construction crew, worrying about the dollars being spent, and *thinking*. This is another sweet spot in small business management, and a very rare one: when the day-to-day is so well executed that the owner can relax and just think. I left each day hours before Pierce and Manuel and spent my evenings in hemp research, buying specialized equipment for later delivery, and planning the next moves on the chessboard.

Very few people in the Hemp Space knew what this kind of operation might cost, but we were all discovering in real time what it *did* cost. This was a tiny ten-acre parcel, and the expenses were enormous. I wasn't worried, knowing I'd bill the weedwhackers using some formula later on. The weedwhackers didn't seem concerned either; they were there every day too, saw the scale of the operation, and never once asked about the accruing expenses.

By the middle of September, I was in for over $250,000 in labor, supplies, and machinery. The expenses were showing no sign of letting up, and while my army had done great work setting up our forward base of operations, we hadn't begun the main assault, which was processing 15,000 hemp plants. So far, we hadn't processed even one. Pierce and I were satisfied, though.

We should have remembered the famous dictum of Field Marshal von Moltke, the Prussian military genius: No battle plan survives the first encounter with the enemy.

Chapter 6
HANG 'EM HIGH

Hoophouse 1 was plant-ready, and the split crews were working hard and well. Harvest day was scheduled for September 18. I don't know how word got out but on harvest day about forty people showed up to work. This was partly because the weedwhackers had planted early and other nearby growers wouldn't be harvesting for another couple of weeks, and partly because word had spread that we were paying $20 an hour. The Hemp Space communication network seemed to work like a beehive. The standard wage was $15, but there had been rumblings about a labor shortage, so we agreed to pay $20. The fuel the Hemp Space hive runs on is rumor, but the economy was humming along nicely and the unemployment rate in Colorado was at a historic low, so it made sense to start high.

I wasn't particularly worried about finding workers. All those years I'd spent orbiting the underclass as a long-haul mover had given me deep experience in finding day laborers in unfamiliar towns all over the country. Here's one thing I knew for sure: a rising economic tide doesn't lift all boats. That was the core of the 1980s supply-side mantra, but these aren't actually boats, they're people. Some folks are washed ashore because they have disabilities, some are mentally damaged, and some are too far off the beach to be easily launched. Some simply don't want to launch, others lack the language skills or cultural knowledge to get launched, and some have become unlaunchable through various entanglements with law enforcement. Such individuals aren't even counted in the unemployment figures because they've been written off and forgotten. Add them all up and you have significant numbers of people living on the edge that the economy—good, bad, and most certainly indifferent—just doesn't touch. Every village, town, and city in America has these folks, and I figured they would become our labor pool. Our work offering had all the allurements: it was short-term, paid in cash, required no job interview, no background check, no language test, and no drug test. Most of our laborers smoked weed all day long while running up and down ladders, standing on scaffolds, and operating heavy machinery. This freaked me out at the beginning but eventually I got used to it. They were good workers.

While our laborers fit the profiles above, they weren't in the main local. They called themselves trimmigrants. I'd seen them in my trucking days. In places like Arcata, California, the town center was awash with scores, sometimes hundreds, of mostly white kids under thirty carrying backpacks and upsetting the local burghers by living in the nearby woods, pissing in alleyways, and dealing small amounts of weed. Trimmigrants are frequently confused with the Rainbow People, a similar nomadic tribe that wanders around America light and rough. No doubt there's a lot of intermingling, but the main difference is that trimmigrants work for a living trimming marijuana or hemp plants and go wherever their skills are required. Trimmigrant central is Mendocino County, California, where an estimated 150,000 workers are needed every October—known as Croptober—to harvest the cannabis crop. With the passage of the Farm Bill allowing hemp cultivation, many trimmigrants moved on to places like Boulder County to check out the new scene. These folks were trickling onto the farm, talking to Pierce, and asking when work was going to start. Pierce told them it was any day now.

The first harvest day broke sunny and clear, and our forty workers punched in at 8 a.m. ready to hang hemp. Our deal with the weedwhackers was that they were to cut the plants and deposit them in front of the hoophouses. After that the plants were our responsibility and our billing for services would begin.

Pierce had his speech ready. This was the second major task he'd been hired for, but I wasn't sure how it was going to go. He didn't have any experience as a crew boss. I certainly hadn't given him any guidance. Pierce brought the crew together, drew himself up to full height, and gave it to them like a coach before the big game:

"Nice to see you all here. Welcome. As you know, we're paying $20 an hour. It's the same for everyone. I'm your crew boss and I make less than you all do. You'll be paid in cash at the end of each day. We'll be getting going as soon as the plants arrive. This is Manuel next to me. He's my number two and speaks fluent Spanish. If you have questions bring them to the two of us. You'll have one fifteen-minute break before lunch. Lunch is at 1 p.m. and is thirty minutes. In the afternoon you'll get another fifteen-minute break. That's it. Otherwise, you'll be working. If you smoke cigarettes, I get it, but smoke during your breaks. We're all adults here and I expect you to police yourselves. We've got more people than we need right now so if you're not holding up your end, we'll figure it out and release you. We've got a great project here which will be providing work for several months. We're nice people so don't screw it up for yourselves. Any questions?"

"Where do we shit and piss?"

"There's a porta-potty over there by the trees. Treat it like it's yours because it is. Please don't use the woods."

They all did anyway.

"Can I set up my tent and stay here?"

"Boulder County says no. Our official policy is to follow all county regulations. On the other hand, we're extremely busy and we won't be trolling the property looking for tents. If there's a complaint or the sheriff shows up, we'll comply with the law."

"Does that mean we *can* stay here?"

"Next question."

"Can we smoke weed?"

"As far as I understand it, the personal use of cannabis is allowed in Colorado on private property."

"Can we smoke weed on the job?"

"Next question."

There weren't any.

Pierce had completely covered all the relevant human resources concerns in the Hemp Space in less than three minutes. An unofficial tent site, a toilet, allowed to smoke weed, and paid every day in cash. It wasn't complicated. His speech had set the right tone. It was a nice opening morning and everyone seemed pumped to get to work.

Another sticky American myth is that of the redoubtable yeoman farmer who toils sunrise to sunset to support his family. That may or may not have had any truth to it, but if anyone in the Hemp Space I knew ever saw a sunrise it was from watching their day end, not begin. The weedwhackers started their plant cutting at 10 a.m., so I had the privilege of paying my army for two hours ($1,600), watching them sit together in a big circle, roll joints, argue over meager honors, and spread rumors. Aside from the joints, the scene resembled nothing so much as a truck stop coffee counter.

After they finally got to work, the cutting went quickly. A weedwhacker holding an actual mechanical weedwhacker with a steel cutting blade nipped off the stalk about an inch from the ground and a tractor pulling a high-sided trailer went behind and workers tossed the trees into the trailer. Mature hemp plants are called trees in the jargon because they're big. The average height was about five feet. It took only about ten minutes to fill the trailer, and they dumped the load onto a tarp in front of the hoophouse. Our army then pulled the tarp to the far end and handed the trees to the hangers who were standing by on scaffolds. The hangers looped the fat end of the stalk into one of the hanging knots and let the tree dangle upside down. Six trees per rope.

With all this transient labor, the farm was starting to look like a campground. We already had Jake and his family in his trailer in permanent residence. There was also a squatter on the land who worked at the convenience store next door to the farm. He was a recent arrival and, with the consent of the weedwhackers, had gathered up the worldly wealth he'd scattered around the county and shown up with a tow truck pulling his inoperable school bus, three dogs, a couple of goats, and, unbelievably, a draft horse. A few days later, a young woman from Mendocino showed up in her 1977 Winnebago RV and asked where she could park. We put her in a quiet corner where she immediately set up a solar shower in the trees and a couple of picnic tables out front. I think she had a side business as tavern keeper and shower provider, but I never bothered to nail it down. Then there was Ian, who explained to anyone who asked, and to those who didn't, that he was a horror film producer from Hollywood between jobs. Ian had a tent but preferred to sleep in the hoophouse alongside "his" plants, where he talked to them throughout the night. Kurt was a former senior executive at a big furniture chain. "It's a great company. They gave me so many chances, but I was in the clutches of demon rum. They didn't want to fire me, but they had to. I understood that. I've a wife and two kids. They're staying with her parents while I pull myself together. Pierce got me this job from the shelter and I'm happy to have it."

There were so many others coming and going we didn't bother to count how many people were living on the farm. Our only real guide was the porta-potty and the bills for toilet paper, which were colossal. The trimmigrants tried, in their ineffective way, to be unobtrusive and respectful. They were exclusively young, white, and educated—basically, living an adventure. Their lifestyle was a choice. The immigrant workers and the mentally ill were another story. These people were just barely keeping it together living in tents and making a day wage. A surprising thing was that most of them were pretty satisfied out on the farm. The fall weather was great, everyone got along, there was money every day, and no cops. I heard more than once that this was a bucolic setting and a vast improvement on the urban homeless environment, which was rife with violence, hard drugs, and police harassment. People were always coming to Pierce and me saying they'd love to stay and work through the winter. It broke my heart.

Processing hemp is a social workplace and there was plenty of opportunity for chitchat. The immigrants, aside from living in terror of discovery, were intently focused on their goals. They had responsibilities back home they were taking care of here. The convenience store down the street did a solid trade sending money orders to countries all over the world. As for the mentally ill, well, we got into some interesting conversations; their coherence astonished me, as did their general lack of medical care. The American

Dream has a lot to answer for if a tent and a day's pay among friendly faces constitutes all that someone with a mental illness can wish for.

We later discovered that a robust social scene developed after hours. Thousands of empty beer cans accumulated in the dumpster, along with a few spent vodka bottles. This was more out of politeness than concealment, I think. Evidently the young woman's Winnebago Tavern and Shower Emporium was a thriving enterprise. I do love an entrepreneur. The trash cans we had distributed throughout the property were always full of used nitrile gloves, water bottles, and hemp stalks. No need to toss beer cans there when they could toss them into the giant dumpster. No need to hide the behavior either. Why bother?

I'd figured the porta-potty would last a month, but it filled in less than a week—even with all the crapping in the woods. I had to arrange for more frequent service calls. Our regular serviceman, Tadziu, was a luminous figure and always in a great mood. He'd come to America from Poland in the late 1980s and spoke pretty good English with a heavy accent. Whenever he drove in with his honey truck, he honked his horn incessantly like he was the ice cream man.

"It's Tadziu!" Everyone loved him and they loved hearing the horn honk. It became a thing. The whole population would stop working and surround his truck, offering him joints, water bottles, beadwork bracelets, and hand-rolled cigarettes.

"Yo Tadziu, wassappeneen?"

"Hi people! Time to clean the tank. You all been good?"

"Yes! We've been good. We've been waiting for you."

I took him aside one day and asked him about the connection he had with the community.

"I honk, yes. People *love* to see me. I like to let them know I'm here. Clean shitter coming. Sound simple and *is* simple until shitter is full. Then things get complicated. The smell you get used to, OK? No big thing. I think my shit smell too, but better than porta-potty. Human being get used to anything almost. Best thing in life is to see people smile when you show up."

I asked him the secret to his radiance.

"In Poland," he said, "people not happy to see me. I have bad job. Have PhD in industrial engineering from Krakow University of Technology. I look for inefficiency in factory. See everywhere. Make suggestion first, then order. Nobody obey. Big stress. Me big problem. This better. I simple man. Work hard cleaning porta-potty, make OK money, provide for family. Not great money, but I'm Santa Claus who don't work Christmas. Every other day I bring gift to many people. This interesting place here. I like it. I go mostly to construction places, stadiums. Nobody say 'hello Tadziu' and give me cigarette. Nobody notice me at all mostly. Invisible. Nice to be treated like human being. That's reason I honk horn. Like elk honk in forest look for other elk. I honk for human being. Here you have them. Many people here live invisible too. I understand."

——

Manuel had been keeping a close eye on the trusses and when Hoophouse 1 was about a third full, he pulled me aside and showed me his notebook.

"Would you mind looking at this?"

"I see a bunch of As and Bs and Xs."

"Look at the number at the end."

"It's negative."

"It's a quadratic equation, gringo. You understand, right?"

"Not one bit. Are you speaking Spanish?"

"I might as well be. Didn't you take any math at your fancy college?"

"I took geology. Rocks for jocks. I was never a science guy."

"I didn't learn this at school either. I picked this up in jail. They had a 1979 algebra book in the library. I was the only guy to ever check it out. It had just sat there for years. It helped pass the time."

"And?"

"And what? Why was I in jail? Long story and not important. As far as the algebra goes, A is the downward pressure calculated by the weight of the plants, B is the truss strength taking into account the columns we installed. I solved for the C coefficient."

"This isn't Spanish. This is Greek. What does all that mean?"

"It means our hoophouses are going to collapse if we don't increase B."

"We need more columns."

"Excellent pupil, gringo. You're slow but you finally got it. We need to put columns on every single truss, not every other one. And we have to double up every 2x4 and make it a 4x4."

"I thought you'd already figured this out?"

"I made an educated guess given the available information. Time to recalculate. Would you mind going to Boulder Lumber? I've got a list of some stuff."

I went off to Boulder Lumber in a great mood. I had an Einstein here in Manuel who wasn't afraid to admit a mistake, and Pierce was running the crews with perfect hard and soft pressure. It's the small businessman's dream.

Why was Manuel working for me at $25 an hour? He could have been running a space shuttle launch. Think about the human potential lost to our country by people like Manuel being pigeonholed into a certain trajectory. Part of the myth of the American

Dream is that you have the freedom to rise above that trajectory and pull yourself up by your bootstraps. Oh yeah? Maybe if you have superhuman drive. Maybe if you have the strength of character to overcome the defeatism of your own cultural pressures born out of racism and condescension. Maybe if you have someone who can tell you there are scholarships and grants available to continue your education. Maybe if you have a role model who makes smart decisions in his daily life you can observe and emulate. That's an awful lot of *maybe if*s.

What I do know is that Manuel was thriving on this project. I'd known him a long time and this wasn't the first time I wished I could give him something more than just temporary work. In human terms he was not reaching his potential, and in economic terms he was an underperforming asset. There are millions of people like this in America. They're losing themselves and we're losing them. It's not what a healthy society does.

Meanwhile, we had hoophouses to buttress. Manuel pulled the construction crew off Hoophouse 2 and set them to installing the new columns in Hoophouse 1 before it collapsed. This was no small feat where the plants were already hanging, but Manuel led the guys through the jungle of hemp trees with ladders and lumber and put them up. The hoophouses didn't fall down, which was the important part. A friend of mine up the road had his hoophouse collapse during hanging. Nobody was hurt but he had to take out all his plants, reinforce the building, and rehang. More money.

It took three days to fill Hoophouse 1 with 4,500 plants. Then it was a waiting game to see how the plants would dry. It was slow going, even though there were two massive fans at the end of the building that we kept going twenty-four hours a day. To speed things up we put in four more giant fans ($2,000) midway, and supplemented those with another fifty small fans ($2,500) on the floor facing up. There was no electrical power at the farm, so I bought two more 9,000-watt generators ($1,500), bringing our power fleet to five. Six when you count the generator for Jake's camper. This was a long way from the bucolic eagles and horses I was with when quietly staking out hoophouse locations. Between the generators, the workers, and the traffic in and out, the place was loud. It was in fact, an industrial site, as all farms are.

Boulder Lumber was our go-to place for wood, but it was Murdoch's, the farm and ranch store, where we went for almost everything else. The sales folks at Murdoch's started calling me by name and led me around with a second cart, always steering me well clear of the hat department. My daily trips for supplies were running at least $1,000 a visit, and I wasn't by any means the only hempster going in there and dropping big coin. It was illuminating to watch how quickly Murdoch's, normally a red-neck sanctuary, absorbed the Hemp Space into its orbit. This rapid normalization is the reality whether you're in Medellin, Manzanilla, or Mendocino. Local businesses don't see their farm customers as criminals. They're neighbors and colleagues and their kids play soccer together. I very much doubt that farmers south of the border are overly concerned about the effects of their produce on gringo drug users thousands of miles away. And why should they be? The US wants these farmers to stay poor so some Yanqui can't snort his lines on a Friday night in the Olive Garden men's room while watching the playoffs? No thanks, amigo. We'll plant what we plant. Why don't you go back north and clean up your own house?

———

After fixing the columns, we returned the crews to building Hoophouses 2 and 3. I was really starting to hemorrhage money now, with almost forty workers getting paid every day and daily trips to Murdoch's and Boulder Lumber for supplies. It was a full-time job for one worker just to get gas and keep the generators running. I wasn't worried, keeping in mind the eventual payday, but I was burning through $10,000 a day, seven days a week.

The weedwhackers were holding off the rest of their harvest for a couple of days to build up a little more CBD content. Pierce and I were also trying to figure out the other part of our business plan, which was to process plants for other farmers when we were finished with the weedwhackers. This was complicated because we didn't know when the weedwhacker plants would be dry, so we couldn't tell a farmer when we'd be ready. Since all the farmers had a harvest window they had to provide to the CDA, and their plants were getting hot too, nobody wanted to sign up with us unless we could guarantee a date. Compounding the problem was the fact that we couldn't tell a farmer what we would charge them either. Nevertheless, we were in discussions with several farmers nearby.

Pierce and I really wanted to process Billy Held's eight acres just up the road. Billy was interested because he didn't have big hoophouses or bucking and trimming equipment. True to his shoestring roots, at harvest time Billy would hang plants on anything he could find. He'd fill his greenhouses, barn, sheds, and, after they were full, he'd lay plants over his barbed wire pasture fences. I joked with him that if I went inside his house, he'd have plants hanging from his shower curtain bar. He replied, "That's the right way to be thinking, but it's too humid in there. I tried it already. Not that I shower much during harvest. What's the point? The hemp resin doesn't come off until you stop handling plants every day."

Billy knew his method for drying hemp wasn't ideal, but it was certainly the cheapest. He bucked his plants using a hired crew with hand buckers instead of the $33,000 Mother Bucker Munch Machine we had, but that worked for him too, more or less. For trimming, he borrowed or rented a trimming machine or paid trimmigrants to hand-trim perfect buds that he sold at premium prices. He also had his consumer brand and an extraction lab. I don't know how Billy kept all those plates spinning, especially when you could reach him on a busy morning, and he'd spend forty minutes warmly chatting away as if he had the whole day with nothing to do. I liked him a lot.

Billy came by frequently to check out the hoophouse construction and when we got going with the processing he came by even more. I could tell he liked our setup. It was fast, efficient, and produced an excellent product. His method was slow and cheap, but he knew it sacrificed quality. He'd planted his crop two weeks after the weedwhackers, so he wasn't yet ready for harvesting. We thought he'd be the perfect client to have when the weedwhacker stuff was finished and were really hoping Billy would sign up, but since we still had no idea what our costs were to dry, buck, and trim, we didn't know how much to charge. We'd agreed beforehand with the weedwhackers that we'd figure that out later on with their crop, but you can't do business with Billy Held when he doesn't know what he's going to pay. The second challenge was that Billy wanted to know exactly what day he could bring in his plants, if we ever did give him a price. We couldn't do that either. We were at a friendly impasse on both matters, but we still talked every day.

We were also in frequent contact with Tom Ward, a mile or so away, about processing his crop, but most of his was going to CBD extraction for his horse product. Tom was interested in turning the top flowers of his plants (called colas) into smokeable flower, but he wasn't going to sign up with us without a cost sheet or a timetable either.

We met too with Alec next door and ran into the same two problems. "What's it going to cost and when can we harvest?"

Obviously, there would be no additional processing deals until we got those two details ironed out. We were getting closer on the cost end because I was running daily expense tallies, but we were cautious. Our fee structure was something we had to get right, or we'd lose money on every pound we processed.

These are the speed bumps any new business goes through, and we had a couple of things going in our favor. First was that unless you were Billy Held, you had to get your crop dried somewhere and it wasn't as if there were barns or hoophouses or warehouses lying around unused. Tom Ward solved that problem by building a large hoophouse on his own farm. (That was the barn that collapsed when he hung a bunch of plants from the roof, but Tom just went to work and fixed it. "I won't do it that way again," was his quiet reflection on the matter. He didn't have a Manuel on staff.) Second was weather. It was getting to the end of September and the threat of an early frost loomed large. Hemp is a rugged plant and can take a lot of weather, but it can't freeze. Think of the tomato plants in your backyard. An hour or two below 32 degrees and your tomatoes are a dead, smelly mess. The same is true for hemp, we were told.

Aside from these concerns, we were finishing the other hoophouses and drying plants in Hoophouse 1. The drying was complicated and time-consuming. Each plant had a different moisture level depending on where in the field it had grown and how much irrigation had been put on it. Inside the hoophouse, despite all the fans, the humidity varied a lot even within a few feet. The plants weren't drying at a uniform rate. We'd been told it would take seven to ten days, but it was taking longer. And this was Colorado. It's a semi-arid climate. How the hell did they dry plants in

Oregon, where it rains all the time? What we did know was that we wouldn't be able to just drag out the dried plants on a first-in first-out basis. We'd have to cherry-pick the rows using a handheld moisture meter and select the right plants at the right time. This meant more time and money, and complicated our cost and time estimates once again.

Finally, though, we had some plants ready for the buckers on September 28. It had been ten days from harvest, and it took that long for even a small portion of the plants to dry. Others were still too wet. We used that time to finish the other hoophouses, so we were ready for the rest of the crop. We'd had gorgeous weather all through September. Dry, with temperatures in the low eighties, making it perfect for work.

For the bucking, the $33,000 Munch Machine Double Mother Bucker I'd purchased had two workstations. The plants were taken down from the ropes by our trimmigrants and dropped into six-by-three-foot heavy-duty cardboard boxes that I'd bought whole-sale from a moving supply company. The boxes full of plants were then wheeled out and dumped onto a pair of four-by-eight-foot tables, where a dozen or so trimmigrants cut the branches from the stalk with hand clippers. The branches were then fed into the Munch Machine feet first and the machine dragged the branch through a hole, stripping off the buds and dropping them into a plastic bin in front.

The stalk and branches were spit out the back end and formed piles that were carted away to a corner of the farm. By harvest end the hemp stalk pile was about twenty feet high and thirty feet in diameter. We tried to find a place to sell it, but there was no market anywhere for hemp stalk. I thought that was a terrible waste, since there must have been some place for the stalks in those 25,000 uses of hemp. At least, the rest of our hemp product—whether burned, eaten, or vaped—disappeared without any waste product. America is often called a consumer culture, but coming from my moving industry heritage, we're not a consumer culture but a transfer culture. Most of our stuff doesn't get consumed. It moves around for a while and then accumulates. When the accumulation hits critical mass, meaning there's no more room in the basement or garage for all the useless stuff we own, off it goes into the mini-storage for a while, and it's then discarded, often by the next generation, who have no use for glass fronted breakfronts, Fletcher Knebel novels, or the needlepoint variations of the Topeka skyline painstakingly stitched by your maiden great-aunt. All these treasures find their resting places in landfills mostly.

My favorite job in what I was starting to see as a hemp flower factory was cutting branches on the big tables and sending them to the Mother Bucker. I'd just stand there and snip, working next to other folks for hours on end so there was lots of time for conversation. I never tire of listening to the life stories of people inhabiting the bottom of the American Dream. Everyone on our crew was flotsam from the traditional economy. One was a finish carpenter and recovering alcoholic, another was an intellectual who admitted to mental health issues. "You know what screwed me up?" he'd ask rhetorically. "Education. I was a philosophy major. The minute I encountered nondualism I fell apart. All you out here think you're functioning? *Functioning?* That's a relative term. We're all here getting day-pay on a hemp farm and we're all losers. None of you are functioning. Maybe you're maintaining, barely, and that's because you don't understand nondualism. If you did, you'd be as messed up as I am. It looks like you all are messed up, but you don't know why. I do. It's nondualism, and that's why I'm smarter than all of you."

He was, needless to say, not the most popular member of the

crew, but I've since looked up nondualism and he has a point. The difference is that his reasonable point doesn't drive me into depression and despair. That makes me stupid or a dualist, I guess.

Another was our resident cannabis/hemp expert with an exhaustive knowledge of all the processes. He was also a certified massage therapist who gave out his expertise gratis to the crew after hours. His cannabis knowledge wasn't theoretical. He had a vape device that transmitted his 80% shatter dose throughout the day. They say you can't overdose on cannabis, and I believe it after watching him. They also say you can't be addicted to cannabis, but I beg to differ. After an hour or so on the scaffolds, he would start to shake and have to drop down and go outside to dab.

Not all the crew were rudderless or homeless. One trimmer from Maryland rented a VRBO condo in Boulder and came to work just for kicks. There was a father-and-son team; the father was an engineer who had earned his heroin medal in Vietnam and spent the next thirty years on the streets. When the Veterans Administration finally admitted that exposure to Agent Orange might have led to real disabilities, he qualified for a subsidized apartment in Boulder. He had only just met his son, whom he'd never known he had. The son had PTSD from his service in Iraq. They were inseparable, always working together as a team, rolling each other's cigarettes and sharing lunch sandwiches. Then we had Eddie from Eritrea, Dave from Ireland, a whole clan from Mexico, Alexa from Mendocino, which *is* also a foreign country, and Conor from Lake Shore Drive in Chicago, another foreign country.

It was a random mix that evolved into a cohesive and productive economic and social unit. Pierce and I can take some credit for creating the environment for a civilized structure to emerge. We were benevolent monarchs. We weren't philosopher-kings because we had no grand vision. Our little society was temporary and had no vision other than to produce quality hemp flower. Maybe that's good enough, and all the big thinkers might think about lowering their sights. From a Buddhist perspective, and definitely from a long-haul mover's perspective, all societies are temporary and grand visions either end up on the ash heap of history or as tourist attractions. I've done the tourist thing, looking upon all these travesties that carry the same old story of myth defining culture. Sure, those fables leave around some nice buildings, paintings, writings, and music, but I generally find the tourist detritus of grand visions as boring and embarrassing to a society as its creation myth. If I was an Egyptian, I wouldn't want anyone to see the pyramids. I mean, there are only three interpretations here. One is that their ancient society knew something really important that their successors carelessly forgot—that's pretty embarrassing. Two is that they squandered massive resources to build ridiculous tributes to what, exactly? That's even more embarrassing. Three is that there was obviously a central government back then that could encourage or coerce many thousands of people into a collective social effort. That's the ultimate embarrassment, since the current government can't even get a Cairo cab driver to obey a traffic light. I'm not picking on the Egyptians here. We're going to have the very same embarrassing problem here in America when future archeologists uncover trillions of square feet of warehouse space and wonder what was so important to our culture that we destroyed our villages, cities, and open space to build these square temples. When those scientists discover that those buildings were filled with whoopee cushions, outdoor furniture, electronics, sex toys, Tupperware, 3XL gray track pants, and five-pound blocks of Tillamook cheese, they're going to wonder what I wonder at Giza: What the hell were these people thinking?

On the other hand, as a tourist I really do enjoy a *failed* grand vision. For example, why hasn't the second tower of the Strasbourg cathedral been built? They've had seven hundred years, for crying out loud. Why doesn't Denver have a beltway around it like every other city in America? Why does a benevolent idea like sharing everything equally between all of us always end in cruelty and massacre? Those are just three, and it can make a fun parlor game to think of more. We discussed these and other interesting questions on the branch cutting line at the hemp factory.

Most of our crew were damaged or troubled in some way. The ones who weren't were mostly women. I'd call them adventurers. There were a half dozen or so, and the tavern keeper with the antique Winnebago was the solid leader. All the women were in their early twenties, professional trimmigrants, taking some time to look over the world and see what it offered. They didn't have much time or patience for the minor-league males hanging around and they made that crystal clear. It never became a problem. The women knew how to take care of themselves and the guys in our crew weren't predators. In fact, no serious incident of any kind happened in the months we processed there, though we did catch one guy stuffing his pockets with hemp buds. He got a quick ride into town and was dropped off at the bus station and that was the end of that.

With our convivial crew, we could buck about 150 pounds an hour of dried plant, which left us with about 75 pounds of flower. Since we had 22,500 pounds of dried plant, we figured it would take about twenty days to buck the whole crop. After bucking, we still had another whole process to perform. The flower in the bins needed to be trimmed into sellable buds, and that takes even longer than bucking. We were looking at a minimum five weeks to finish. That wasn't nearly fast enough, because CBD content degrades quickly, and the buds dry out if left lying around. They can also rehydrate, depending on weather, and produce mold. If there was even trace mold, the crop would become worthless.

We'd established a management meeting with the weed-whackers each morning at 10 a.m. In one of those meetings, they told us our timetable wasn't working and suggested we purchase a second Mother Bucker, which I duly bought for another $33,000. Naturally, this threw off our cost estimates once again. We weren't getting any closer to a price per pound or a time estimate for processing.

After a container from the Mother Bucker was full of flower, it was dumped into open cardboard boxes to cure. Plastic bins don't breathe, but cardboard does. The cured flower was then tested for moisture and, when ready, sent over to the trimming machine. Trimming machines look like a cannon and have a perforated metal barrel with sharp edges. The flower is loaded into the barrel, and it rotates like a clothes dryer and shaves off the remaining leaf material, leaving a nice-looking bud. The residual leaf is captured in a bin and is called trim, which is a sellable product for CBD oil and roll-ups but not nearly as valuable as the buds. Trimming is a skilled occupation. If you trim your flower too long, you get tiny popcorn buds. If you don't trim enough, you get buds with leaf and stem attached called crow's feet. Both affect the sale price of your bud, so the trick is to trim like Goldilocks: just right.

The weedwhackers recommended we buy the $10,000 Triminator XL which, like the Munch Machine Double Mother Bucker was the best on the market. The Triminator could produce buds at about 65 pounds an hour. Our two Mother Buckers could produce about 250 pounds of flower an hour, so there was clearly going to be a bottleneck in trimming. The solution for that was to buy more trimmers, but there wasn't a trimmer available for sale anywhere in the world during that harvest season. The extractors had caught up with their backlog, but the trimming manufacturers were still behind. I back-ordered two more Triminator XLs and rented a couple smaller Triminators. To clear the bottleneck, we decided to run the trimmers in three shifts. Now we had a twenty-four-hour operation going. I'd already rented two 40-foot steel shipping containers and ordered a third, and put lights inside so we could run the trimming operation all night long. It was no problem finding trimmers for these overnight shifts. It's not hard work and the trimmigrant would put on her earbuds—the best trimmers are women, for some reason—groove on her tunes, and dump the load when the buds looked right. There's definitely worse work out there in America—loading and unloading moving trucks, to name one.

We still couldn't get a handle on costs, though, because the curve balls kept coming. There was the twenty grand prepayment for two more Triminators, the rentals, and now we had three shifts running. This wasn't getting us any further with potential clients like Billy or Tom or Alec. I was no closer to giving a client a cost for services or a solid date for plant delivery than I'd been a month ago. It was true that Hoophouse 1 was getting emptied of hanging plants, but in their place were hundreds of cardboard boxes with curing flower. At least we were catching up with around-the-clock trimming.

By the first week in October, we had dialed in the workflow. We were producing hundreds of pounds a day of fine smokeable flower. I'd bought five hundred plastic bins from Sam's Club ($4,000), and we sealed the final product into those 27-gallon containers and handed them over to the weedwhackers to sell. Hemp prices, they said, were still looking good since there had been no new product since last year's harvest.

Hemp prices weren't on our radar. We were doing tactics, not strategy.

Chapter 7
THE BIG FREEZE

At our Saturday, October 5, management meeting, the weedwhackers brought up the weather forecast. There was a cold front coming in, calling for a low of 16 degrees Fahrenheit with snow on Tuesday or Wednesday. We were OK in one respect, because all their plants were now hanging in the hoophouses. Nothing was left in the fields. Still, even hanging plants can't be allowed to freeze. The weedwhackers wanted to know our plan. I told them we didn't have one, but we would. I waited until Monday to make sure the forecast looked real, and it did.

I went down to Boulder at lunchtime and reserved a giant diesel heating unit for the next morning (the kind of thing you see at a tent wedding reception). It sat on a trailer and had connections for three 12-inch-diameter ducts. My plan was to put a duct into each hoophouse, seal the doors, and keep the thing running through the storm with the interior fans going full blast. The storm was expected to start Tuesday afternoon and finish Wednesday morning, giving way to a high of 82 on Wednesday afternoon. So this was just a freak Colorado storm, as often happens. As I was pulling out of the rental shop, my phone rang. It was Billy Held.

"Hey Finn? You've seen the forecast?"

"Yeah, Billy. I just rented a diesel heater. It's big. Something on the form says two million BTUs."

"My crop's still in the ground. I'm harvesting tomorrow. You got room in your hoophouses? I'm ready to dry, buck, and trim with you guys."

"Billy, I don't have pricing for you."

"We can figure that out. I've been watching your operation. You seem like standup guys. I'm going to lose the whole crop if I leave it in the field."

"OK Billy. Bring it over."

"Thanks."

"We'll see if you thank me or not later. The costs are enormous. You've been doing it your own way a long time. I've got a feeling you're not going to like our final number."

"Right now, my final number is zero. Anything above that is looking good."

"OK, then. We'll figure it out later."

This was exactly what Pierce and I had been expecting. Desperation. A few minutes later, I got another call. This time it was Alec and his eight acres next door.

"Did you see the forecast?"

"Yup."

"Got any room in your hoophouses? We're ready to dry, buck, and trim with you guys."

"Sorry Alec. I've got Billy Held coming in with his eight acres tomorrow."

"Ah shit."

"Sorry man. I'd love to help you out, but I don't have any space left."

"Ah shit. Everyone's been counting the pennies and forgot about the dollars."

"I know. You guys were perfect. Right next door. I tried to get the numbers for your boss, but I couldn't, and he wouldn't take the risk. I understand that, but now he's upside down."

"Ah shit."

The looming freeze had lurched everyone out of complacency. Nobody knew whether to shit or go blind. What we needed now were nine hoophouses. We told the weedwhackers Billy Held was coming over the next morning with his crop. That didn't go over well.

"What about our crop?" one asked.

"Hoophouse 1 is holding boxes for curing. We'll stack them to make room for Billy."

"Billy's crop is wet. It's going to humidify the curing buds. We might get mold. Don't you know anything about curing hemp?"

"No, we don't, but we're learning fast. So are you. You make a good point about the humidity. We'll move the curing boxes into one of the storage trailers, set up some propane heaters, and monitor the moisture."

"You said we'd have first dibs on the hoophouses. Now you're setting us aside for a new client. This is our farm. The hoophouses are on our property."

"Remember here that new clients are going to reduce what we'll be charging you. Without new clients, you guys shoulder the whole cost of this enterprise. We're bucking 2,000 pounds a day and trimming in twenty-four-hour shifts, producing another 2,000 pounds daily. We'll be finished with your stuff in a few days. Billy's going to lose his whole crop in the freeze if he can't use the hoophouse."

"We don't like this."

"Neither do we. We had no idea it would be this complicated picking up other growers. Between figuring out costs, and the timing all messed up with drying, nobody wanted to tag on. Now the freeze has everyone looking for us. If you guys say no to Billy's crop, we'll accept that. But it's going to cost you on the back end."

"How much?"

"We have no idea."

"You said you were the business guy who had it all figured out. What's so hard about figuring out a cost per pound?"

"You've been here every day; you've seen how we've been adjusting to the shifting variables. I *am* a business guy, but I never said I *had* it all figured out. I said I *would* have it all figured out, and I will. We've been building the plane as it flies. You told me to order the extra machines, you approved the three shifts for trimming. This is a startup and neither of us knew anything about what it costs to process 15,000 hemp plants. We almost know now, but not quite. What we do know is that the more plants going through the hoophouses, the more it will benefit all of us."

"We still don't like it."

"Do we take Billy's crop or not?"

"Sure. Take it, but we're not happy."

They sure weren't.

We had the trimmigrants load the curing bud into a storage container, and Billy showed up at 9 a.m. the next morning with a convoy of U-Haul trucks. Billy was his usual sunny self. I was sure he'd been up all night getting organized and he must have started cutting plants well before dawn. You'd never know it to talk to him, though. He handed me a coffee and calmly surveyed his crew unloading plants.

"Thanks for doing this. I know I wasn't in your plan."

"It was in our plan to get other growers' plants to process. You were the first to call. Alec next door called literally two minutes after you did. I had to tell him we were full up. Anyway, Billy, I'm happy to do it. Who knows, maybe we'll even make some money together."

"I'm glad you're happy. Me too. Those guys over there don't look happy. They usually come over to say hello. Am I getting the evil eye?"

"Definitely."

"I see. I'm the last-minute plant guy. The cheapskate who wouldn't sign on until the weather got bad."

"Yup."

"Are you sore at me too? Even though you're happy?"

"I'm not sore at all, Billy. It's just business. I wouldn't have signed on with a couple of greenhorns like us either, especially with an open-ended invoice. I've appreciated all your help this year. You and Tom Ward were the only guys who gave us the time of day a million years ago in April. You've been free with advice and you're a nice guy. There aren't that many nice guys in the Hemp Space."

"Are you referring to the evil eyes over there?"

"The weedwhackers? Nah, they're OK. They're scared about this whole thing not working out and that makes them edgy. They've been fine to work with. They never liked you coming around, though. It wasn't anything personal. They just didn't want an experienced grower nosing around and seeing their mistakes."

"I never said a word to them about mistakes, though I saw plenty. But they ended up with great plants. Hemp is not difficult to grow. There's a reason they call it weed. The difficulty is the money it takes. Still, they should be proud."

"Well, they're pissed off at you for jumping in at the last minute and they're pissed off at me for letting you."

"Were you supposed to be exclusive to them?"

"Never. This was always the plan. Sign on other growers as time and space allowed."

"Well, my plants do need a roof. That's business. Still, I don't like to be the cause of conflict between partners."

"We're not their partners. We're their processors. The plants are theirs. Everything else you see here belongs to me."

"What? The hoophouses? The Munch Machines?"

"Everything."

"That's interesting. Who came up with that idea?"

"I guess I did."

"Maybe you can do the same thing on my farm."

"Why don't we see how all this turns out first."

"What are you charging them for drying, bucking, and trimming? I understand you and I have an open deal, but for them you must have figured something out."

"Nope. You have the same deal they do. We'll figure it out when we're finished. I couldn't get any numbers together beforehand. I'm barely putting numbers together now."

"I'm not sure if you're brilliant or crazy. Between you and me, I wasn't the least bit interested in those guys. I wanted to see what you and Pierce were going to do. It's been a pleasure watching you, and especially Pierce, grow into this thing. You watch folks work for a while and you get a sense of their character. I'm impressed. More than impressed. I'm in awe."

"I appreciate that. I'll be sure to tell Pierce."

We went over to the U-Hauls and helped the crew haul Billy's trees into Hoophouse 1.

———

Pierce was supervising the hanging of Billy's crop inside when the clouds started to gather and the temperature dropped. With the big freeze imminent, I went and picked up the diesel heater. Then I went to Tractor Supply and bought a 100-gallon diesel tank ($400) and drove to a truck stop and filled it with red diesel ($350). Red diesel is farm fuel which you can buy without any of the road taxes included—it's dyed red so it can be identified as tax-free fuel. God help an over-the-road truck driver caught with red diesel in his tank.

I backed the heater up midway between the three hoophouses, then cut a hole in the vinyl wall of each one and inserted a 12-inch-diameter hose, sealing the hole with white duct tape. The gray tape was cheaper, but the white looked better. (Just because you're in a crisis doesn't mean you lower your standards.) Pierce and the crew were just finishing for the day, and he'd released the second and third trimming shifts because of the storm. He offered to stay and help with the heater, but I turned him down.

"You've been going at it hard, Pierce. I'm going to take this one. It's an all-nighter, but it only needs one person. Go home and get some sleep. I'm going to need you fresh in the morning."

"Are you sure? There's nobody else here. It's going to get really quiet."

"It won't get that quiet with the heater running like a blast furnace. What do you mean, nobody else here? There's a couple dozen people living in tents all over the place."

"They're all gone. A bunch went to the shelter in Boulder. The others figured out alternative cribs. This storm is going to be a real bitch. Even the horror movie producer split. I saw him saying goodbye to the plants. He said a prayer. He even went into Hoop-house 1, welcomed Billy's new plants into the fold, and apologized that he wouldn't be here to ease them through their first night. That was nice."

"Great. Maybe I'll get some sleep then."

"I don't like this at all. What if something happens?"

"Like what?"

"My mind reels with bad possibilities."

"Go reel at home. I'm doing this and you're not."

"See you in the morning then."

"Nighty-night. I'll be fine."

I fired up the heater and crawled through each hoophouse to check the air flow. It made a good warm breeze, but each hoop-house was 40,000 cubic feet, about the same space as nine tractor trailers. The forecast said the low that night would be 16 degrees Fahrenheit, and each hoophouse needed to stay well above freezing. That was a lot of space to heat, and it wasn't like they were insulated. There was only a vinyl sheet between the weather and the plants. I should have asked Manuel to give me a heat transfer calculation, but I didn't think of it. I just went and rented the biggest and baddest diesel heat generator I could find.

Manuel was still working for us, bucking branches on the Munch Machines. We didn't need any more Einstein work, and he'd put away his specialized tool bags and joined the ranks as a day laborer. He was back to being a private instead of a colonel. He seemed content, but then he always did. I never figured out what Manuel was thinking about anything. Maybe he was a bucket of equanimity, a seething froth of resentment, or something in between. I'll never know. There will always be a cultural divide between us. Sure, we can work together, have some fun, drink some beers, joke around, get angry at each other and patch things up, but people are tribal and I don't blame Manuel any more than I blame my own Irish clan. We don't let folks in either.

I filled the heater with diesel from my spanking new fuel tank, fired it up, set the temperature to high, and drove home to gear up for the long night ahead. The snow had started. I threw a sleeping bag, two headlamps, and five Clif Bars into the truck and changed into my backcountry ski outfit. Insulated rubber boots, heavy socks, long johns, underlayer, bib, flannel shirt, wool sweater, cashmere scarf, wool hat, glove liners, Kinco mittens, and my Descente ski jacket. I had to fish all that out from my ski bin in the attic. It was early October, for Crissakes!

I rushed back to the farm, worried about the fuel level, but saw I'd get about four hours of heat between fills. It was now 8 p.m., the snow was really falling, and the temperature was dropping fast.

When I turned off the heater to fill the fuel tank at midnight, it was 20 degrees outside. Pierce was right about it getting quiet. The silence was an ear-splitting roar of absolutely nothing. It dawned on me that I'd never been here at night. As I pumped the fuel from my 100-gallon tank into the heating unit, the hoop-houses loomed above me through the snow in what appeared to be a distinctly menacing profile. The 12-inch hoses going into their sides looked like anacondas, or maybe large intestines. It hadn't occurred to me that all the squatters would decamp or that I might miss them. It hadn't occurred to me that being here in a snow-storm alone all night might be unsettling.

After I filled the fuel tank and started up the heater again, it was time to check the temperature inside the hoophouses. I had bought fifteen thermometers the day before and taped five inside each hoophouse at random spots. Time to make the rounds. My plan was to visit each thermometer, mark the temps in a little notebook I'd brought, and adjust the hoses and fans if needed. I rolled up the door of Hoophouse 3 about a foot so I could crawl inside, and rolled it down again. I had to crawl because the jungle of hemp plants was hanging only an inch or two off the floor.

The sense of menace only increased as I made my way toward the thermometers. I had my headlamp on, and it gave out a feeble light. All the fans were running full speed, which made the plants sway in slow, random pirouettes. I could hear them moving against one another with a low hiss, and the shadows they cast looked terrifying, like thousands of dead bodies swinging from nooses. I tried to ignore them and remember where I'd put the thermometers but I couldn't. I finally found a couple of them, saw they were above freezing, wrote the temperatures with a shaking hand in my notebook, and got the hell out of there.

I was thankful for the noise of the heater, and when it was time to shut it off to refill the fuel tank at around 3:30 a.m., I stood there almost frozen. I was afraid to turn it off and face the silence. I knew all I'd hear was the snow falling, which you can't really hear, but you can. When I finally did turn the heater off, it was time for round two of temperature testing. God help me, I didn't want to go back in there.

This time it was worse. I was being watched. There was something *aware*, alive, dead, I didn't know. I crawled between the hanging plants, looking for thermometers, losing my way, forgetting what I was doing, only knowing something was there. These trees, alive a few days ago, had been murdered. They were screaming in pain for water, sunshine, their root system, their *essence*. I felt the soul of every single dead plant and each one was blaming *me*. They weren't just in agony, they were angry. The menace was palpable, real, terrifying. The horror!

I took a reading from one thermometer. Then I stood up and

ran in a panic, tossing trees aside and screaming. I pushed the specters away from me as they congregated in an enveloping swarm, trying to twist themselves around my neck and finish me off. I ran in every direction with no sense at all except full-on panic. By some kind of providence, I banged into the roll-up door, ducked underneath, and bolted out into the snowstorm. I ran a long way and then fell on my face in a fallow field, gasping.

I had planned to spend the night in one of the hoophouses near a heating duct with my sleeping bag, but I'd have jumped off a bridge before doing that. I wasn't going back in there. Let them all freeze, let their value drop to nothing, let my business go broke. I didn't care. Nothing would induce me back into that abattoir.

I went to my truck, put down the seat and tried to relax. No dice. The proximity of the menace was still too strong. I drove to the convenience store down the road and parked there. I finally calmed down a little bit and realized I still had my notebook in my left hand. I had scribbled something that looked like 45 degrees on my last foray into the abyss. I guess I'll call that success.

I'm a materialist to the core, but the feeling of all those hanging hemp plants reminded me of Sequoia National Park. I suspect the life force of trees is on such a different spectrum from ours that we don't usually notice it. With really giant trees, though, we can feel it a little bit. I felt a palpable sense of consciousness from those sequoias, and it held not just vitality but an undercurrent of menace, too. My night in the charnel house of dead hemp was similar. Maybe it was a vortex of suffering concentrated into a confined area. Both experiences awoke a primal terror inside me.

I was startled back into *this* reality by a sheriff's deputy knocking gently on my truck's window just after dawn. I was still in the convenience store parking lot. The morning was sunny and clear.

"Are you OK, sir?"

"Yes, thanks officer. Bad night."

"Too much fun? Decided to sleep it off?"

"No fun at all. I work at the farm next door. I spent the night keeping the furnace going so the plants didn't freeze."

"That hemp farm?"

"Yes sir."

"I can see you're not drunk or hung over, but you're a mess."

"I am. That's why I came over here. I got seriously spooked."

"You can't sleep here in your car. Time to move along."

"I agree, sir. Thanks. I'll just be driving to the farm there."

"Be careful. You don't look right."

"I'm not. It's the trees talking to me."

"Sure it is. Trees talk all the time. This is Boulder, Colorado. I was having a chat with my dogwood just the other day. Want to know how I knew it was a dogwood?"

"Sure."

"By its bark."

The deputy was doing his best to commiserate with yet another Boulder County weirdo. Most of the law enforcement officers around here are quick on their feet and have a sense of humor. They have to operate within the wacky culture without being part of it.

"What did the dogwood say to you?" I asked. His joke had gone right over my head.

"It wasn't really talking. I was trying to be funny. Trees don't talk. Move along."

I went over to the farm and looked at the hoophouses. They had some overnight snow on the roofs, and I wondered if Manuel had calculated that extra weight. The temperature was rising fast, and the snow began cascading off the roof. I held my breath, expecting at any moment that all three buildings would collapse.

Pierce arrived fresh and ready for work.

"How did the night go?"

"Just fine. It dropped inside to about 45 degrees. No freezing."

"Long night?"

"I'd rather not talk about it. Better you weren't there."

"Tell me about it sometime."

"Nah. Nothing special." Then I went home to bed.

———

Did I say that running a small business is fun? Well, it is. I *love* this. I didn't love the trees that night, but solving business problems effectively gives me a rush I get nowhere else. Toss in some personal inconvenience, like crawling through hoophouses with dead things gripping at my vitals, and I'm near nirvana—at least I am once the fear subsides. Knowing I'd reserved the diesel heater on Monday gave me another boost. When I picked it up, the counter guy told me I was lucky I reserved it because they completely sold out Monday afternoon. Every hemp grower on the Front Range with a barn or a hoophouse was trying to rent one. I wasn't lucky; I was smart. In business, as Branch Rickey said about baseball, "Luck is the residue of design." When your design aligns with reality, it's an amazing feeling.

Pierce and I had expected last-minute demand from growers for processing, and that happened. We didn't expect an early freeze; that was dumb luck. That we were ready and prevented the weedwhacker crop, and Billy's, from freezing, was quick footwork. I know this sounds self-congratulatory, but nobody else will be patting us on the back. That's another small business thing: when you screw up, there's no shortage of people pointing it out, but when you succeed, that's just you doing your job.

Strangely enough, it turned out to be wasted effort. The notion that hemp plants shouldn't freeze is one of those universally accepted precepts that were indicative of the lack of solid knowledge so rife in the Hemp Space. Sometime later I had a chat with Colin Gallagher of Solari Hemp in Longmont, the most professionally managed hemp enterprise I encountered. The company was founded by Jake Salazar, one of those sixteenth-century Salazars who received a land grant from the Spanish king Karl V. Jake knew cannabis. He had opened some of the first dispensaries in Denver, sold them, and entered the Hemp Space. Colin grew up in Boulder, went to UNC in Greeley, and earned a master's degree in finance from the University of Denver. He's also a CPA. His family owns a chain of stores called Smoker Friendly. They have almost nine hundred stores nationwide.

I asked him whether his crop had gotten caught in that October freeze.

"It did. We were caught off guard like everyone else. We had a chief science officer on staff, though. While he understood that the freeze would kill the plants, it was harvest time anyway, so he considered it no big deal. We didn't panic. We knew there wouldn't be any further increase in the CBD content because of the freeze, but, according to him, it wouldn't do any other harm and it didn't."

"How do you know that for sure?"

"We had our own Light Lab portable testing setup from Orange Photonics in New Hampshire. Our science guy was testing plants every day before and after the freeze. We saw no deterioration of CBD. I know this goes against everything you've heard, but all you had was rumor. We had data."

While everyone in the Hemp Space was in a frenzy to plant, Solari was the only company I knew that worked the problem in reverse. First, they got their sales channels figured out and then determined how much product they'd plant to correspond to what their sales channels could handle. At each step of the way, they were merciless about capital requirements and costs. They turned down outside money, offered their business partners equity in Solari, and even invented a hemp harvesting machine. They planted 150 acres of hemp outside Eaton, Colorado, the same year we planted. They also had a few acres in Longmont which served as their experimental farm.

"It sounds like you guys had it all figured out."

"We thought we did. We made some big mistakes, too. We didn't account for some of the bad players who had entered the Hemp Space. We had too much trust. We paid $560,000 for a state-of-the-art radio frequency drying machine. Two years later, we're still waiting for it. That was a big hit. Having your plants freeze is OK, but you can't leave them out there forever. Losing the half million dollars was bad enough, but without the dryer, we had half a million plants that ended up rotting in the field. That was worse. Plus we had bottlenecks in the extracting process."

"Everyone did."

"Everyone did, but what we did have were sales channels for our consumer products. We had twenty-two different SKUs, were in three thousand stores, and had our own direct-to-consumer website."

"How much did you grow the following year?"

"Zero. We didn't put a single seed in the ground. We had enough product left over that was properly stored. Good stuff, 10–12% CBD and completely compliant."

"So you're solid now?"

"We'll be OK. Covid messed things up again. We had signed up for twenty-five trade shows. We knew a lot of companies had imploded and the marketplace would be smaller. We were already in a lot of doors and had a track record to show we could execute.

We were looking to land a big fish, like Walgreen's or Circle K. When Covid hit, all the trade shows were canceled. This is a tough business."

"You're staying in it?"

"I am. I'm not always sure why. I'm thirty-five and have two young kids. It's like having three full-time jobs. Maybe I'm just a stubborn Irishman."

"Is there any other kind?"

Chapter 8
WHAT A COUNTRY!

We finished trimming the weedwhacker crop on October 30 and started bucking Billy's and another farmer's small crop on Halloween. Now it was time to tot up all the expenses and figure out what kind of bill to present. While I had a general idea about how much money we were spending and we ran daily expense chits, I had been tossing receipts into a box and depleting my retirement account. It was long past time to clean that up, so I went in a search of an accountant–bookkeeper. This wasn't how I usually operated. Under normal circumstances, I would have had an accountant before a name or even business cards. But we'd been in a frenzy since late August, and I'd had no time.

I stopped in at an accounting firm on Main Street in Longmont to see if they'd be interested in putting our affairs in order. I have a soft spot for Main Street retailers, having been one in several different towns. I've opened and closed thirteen stores in my career. The first one was in the back alley I mentioned earlier and the last one was a luxury cashmere store on the main drag in Greenwich, Connecticut. The rent on that first one was $350 a month and for the last one it was $12,000 a month. It's counterintuitive, but I made more money paying the latter than the former. I remember asking the landlord in Greenwich why the rent was so expensive, and he said, "It's not expensive, it's valuable." It took me a long time opening retail stores in low-end locations to completely understand the truth of that, but the penny dropped while I was reading a biography of Willie Sutton, the legendary bank robber. After being convicted yet again, the judge addressed him from the bench: "Why do you keep robbing banks, Mr. Sutton?"

Sutton thought for a moment and replied: "Well, judge, that's where the money is."

I also had three stores on Nantucket Island, and all were successful. One of them lasted seventeen years. The rents there were also "valuable."

Main Street retailers nationwide have been having a tough time creating a niche between big-box stores and Amazon. It's heartbreaking. Most Main Street businesses are owner-operated, usually by a local who's part of the community. They're being exterminated by what appear to be lower prices and more convenience. Whether that's true or not depends how you value certain intangibles. Some assets are difficult to value, like employing locals with better pay and benefits than the big-boxes, keeping historic buildings occupied, having a pleasant downtown with a mix of offerings making it a place you're proud of, and keeping the expenses and revenue close to home instead of all that money being wire-transferred every night to some faraway place. Communities pay for those "low prices" in ways that seriously degrade the character of their town and the quality of life for everyone. When the Boy Scouts or the local high school decide to raise some funds for a project, the kids descend on the local Main Street retailers for donations—and meanwhile, their parents are buying the clothes and sports equipment at the Walmart on the edge of town. It's easy for a kid to walk into Bill's Barber Shop, or Joe's Tacos, or Karen's Fabrics and ask for something. It's quite another thing for a kid to seek (or get) a donation from a big-box store.

So I just walked in one morning to this Main Street accounting firm and asked to speak to the owner. They had a storefront on the street so people *would* walk in, so people *would* ask for the owner, so that we could meet and talk and get acquainted. I was welcomed inside and ushered into the owner's office. After a few pleasantries, we got down to business. It's possible that these more personal kinds of business arrangements can take up more time than an online intro, but that's not always true. Even if it were, I wouldn't rate that intangible as an inconvenience. To me, inconvenience is waiting twenty minutes on the phone with a call center, and when someone finally gets on the line, they spout a bunch of platitudes from a script they're required to follow, which never seems to directly address my problem. Instead of that frustrating waste of time, I spent the same twenty minutes in an informative discussion with my prospective accountant. He told me about his kids and why he was on Main Street, and I told him about moving from town onto a farm, and he told me farming's tough around here, and I told him Longmont seemed like a nice place to raise a family. This might sound banal, but it was pleasant, and make no mistake, we were also doing business, getting a read on each other, looking for common ground and possible red flags. I believe it's called human interaction. Toward the end of our conversation, I handed him a signed copy of my book about long-haul trucking. I wasn't at all sure how he'd take to my hemp enterprise, and thought I'd preempt any suspicion by establishing some credibility as a published author. The book handover completed, the grateful thanks accepted, I got to it at last.

"We're not growing hemp on my farm. We're in the hemp post-harvest processing business. We have buildings and machinery down in Boulder."

"I've heard a little bit about hemp. Boulder County is supposed to be some sort of hemp vortex. I don't have any hemp clients. I'm not for or against, mind you, I just don't know what's going on. You don't really fit the profile of a dope dealer. No hemp business has come in and asked us to do their books."

"Then I'll be the first to ask. It is a hemp vortex here since it became legal to grow. The Colorado Department of Agriculture thinks hemp might reverse the farming decline."

"I know quite a bit about that. I have lots of farm clients. It's not good out there."

"No, it's not. Maybe hemp will help. It's like a lot of agricultural products in that it needs significant post-harvest processing to become a commercial product. That's what we do."

"Sounds pretty normal."

"It is. If you take us on as a client, it might take a while for your staff to clean things up. My receipts are a mess and I've gone through three different banks in two months."

"We're used to receipts in shoeboxes. We bill by the hour, and messy records from business owners are common. We'll be happy to sort it all out."

"There are going to be lots of cash transactions, more than usual."

"We can work through that. What we can't work through is any funny business. We're strictly on the level here. Anything starts to smell bad, you're out. I live in this town, and I won't be involved in anything except proper business behavior."

"I live here too and that suits me perfectly. We're a legitimate business doing legitimate commerce and we want proper accounting. I've run all my businesses strictly by the book, not least because I need to know if I'm making money or not."

"Sounds good. We'll assign you a bookkeeper. She'll be linked to your accounts and will be your point of contact. Let's clean it all up."

What a relief! We really needed to get the books in order. Not just to know exactly what we'd been spending, but also because the deal we'd made with the weedwhackers was that our finances would be wide open to them when it came to getting paid and I wanted to give them a professional set of books to review.

One thing that made our accounting easier was that all we had were expenses. This was pointed out to me a couple weeks later by the bookkeeper assigned to our account. After going through the receipts, she looked up at me and said, "There's no revenue here."

"I'm glad you noticed that. I'm aware of that too."

"Will there be some revenue?"

"I certainly hope so." There was an awkward silence.

"Good, it's not really a business if there's no income."

"Thanks. I know that. I'm expecting some revenue soon."

Another awkward silence.

"That's what everyone says."

She was my kind of bookkeeper. Give it to me straight and firm with a dollop of skepticism.

Having the accounting set up was wonderful. Banking was another matter entirely. Finding a bank willing to do business in the Hemp Space was a recurring nightmare. Even though the Farm Bill made hemp federally legal, marijuana still wasn't. Regardless of any state's rules allowing marijuana sales in various forms, a bank that had FDIC insurance, which was all of them, wouldn't service marijuana accounts. By extension, mostly having to do with bankers' inherent caution, none of them would go anywhere near the Hemp Space either. Banks saw them as linked industries and were fearful of losing their FDIC coverage, and being assessed big fines if they were caught working, even peripherally, with an enterprise that handled a federally illegal product.

I had set up an LLC for a different business two years before and had an active commercial bank account already at a stolid Midwestern bank. Even back then, I had to sit for an hour or so answering piercing questions about my business. I thought it odd at the time since I'd set up many business accounts before and there had never been an interrogation involved. I explained I was in the moving industry, and we provided labor services to van lines. Long-haul drivers would need laborers and we'd arrange that, pay them, and bill the van line. I explained that day labor was a cash business, that 1099s weren't required for laborers under $600 per person per year, and that what we were doing was legit—which it was. My answer satisfied the banker, and I opened the account. If that had still been my primary business, everything I said then remained true. It was still a little bit true, but most of the truth was that 99% of the funds I was withdrawing were to pay people to build hoophouses and then pay them to process hemp into smokeable flower.

My business was never connected to marijuana, but in September when I started taking out large daily cash withdrawals to pay my army of day laborers, I got a call from the account manager to come in for another chat. I sat down and the banker had my statement in front of her. She asked what exactly my business was, and I told her about providing moving services, and that seemed to end the matter. As the processing business heated up, I was taking out a little less than $10,000 every day. I never took out more, to avoid the IRS 8300 rule that requires cash transactions of $10,000 or more to be reported. A week or so later I got a call from another banker, far beyond Colorado, who said he was with the bank's compliance department at company headquarters. He asked about the large daily withdrawals, and I explained about moving services.

"It looks like your withdrawal pattern is being done to avoid 8300 filings."

"You're right. I am timing my withdrawals to avoid 8300 filings. That's not illegal. I make legal cash withdrawals to provide perfectly legitimate contract labor services to my clients. I'm in the moving and storage industry."

"Do you provide any labor services outside the moving and storage industry?"

Now that was a perceptive question. I wondered how he came up with it. I should have known, but I was in my own business bubble. I figured I was just one guy taking out lots of cash with a good story behind it. Out at company HQ, the computers were no doubt spitting out reports about hundreds of guys like me, all in Colorado, all of whom were, coincidentally, in the middle of a bumper hemp harvest which required lots of cash labor. To the computer algorithm, I was a cog in an easily discernible pattern.

That sharp interrogative from the compliance banker had me approaching an ethical line. I've spent a lifetime in business giving bankers some truth but not the whole truth, which is what they've always given me, but I wasn't going to outright lie.

"We also work in agricultural services."

"What kind of work?"

"We build outbuildings on farms."

"Anything else?"

"We sometimes provide labor for crop processing services."

"What kind of crops?" This guy was no idiot.

"Any kind."

"Cannabis?"

"Cannabis?"

"Marijuana."

"No way. We don't go near that stuff."

"Hemp is cannabis too."

"Is that right?"

"Do you provide labor for hemp processing?"

"Here and there."

"We don't service hemp accounts at this bank."

"I understand that. I probably wouldn't either. Fortunately, we're not a hemp account. We're a labor and service supplier."

"And I understand that distinction. Thanks for your time."

"Thank *you*."

The next morning when I went to the branch for my daily $9K, the manager took me aside and told me my account had been closed. She said she didn't know why, and her records indicated that a cashier's check had been issued yesterday for my balance and sent by FedEx. I'd have my money tomorrow. She looked embarrassed and went off to deal with, no doubt, some other inconvenient banking complication.

Now I can understand, in a way, if you're a bumpkin from a bovine bank based in the backwater boondocks, that you'd want hands off anything to do with hemp. What I can't forgive is that bland bureaucrat, knowing he was going to cut me off, letting me swing in the wind. He could have told me then and there that we were done. I wouldn't have liked it, and we might have had words, but I would have had some respect for his candor.

It was an awkward day over at the farm when the workers lined up to get paid and Pierce had to tell them all they'd all get paid tomorrow. The folks working for us generally didn't have much financial cushion. A day's pay often meant a day's food and the accepted convention in the Hemp Space was to get paid at the end of each day's work.

Our labor relations were already strained. The week before, Pierce had informed the assembly that the hourly wage was going from $20 an hour to $15. This was done unilaterally after a visit from several hemp farmers in the area. They came in a small posse of pickup trucks, raising dust over our nice plants and parking in a line.

The spokesman emerged out of the dust wearing brand new Filson overalls with no shirt, two sleeve tattoos, and a Patagonia cap. He walked up to Pierce figuring he was El Jefe, Pierce being the tallest and carrying the aura of authority.

"Yo, word on the street is you're paying $20 an hour. The going rate is $15."

"Yo? How about hello? I'm Pierce. I'm running the processing here. What can I do for you fellas? Got any names?"

"You can call us the Neighborhood."

"I know the neighborhood. I know Alec and Tom and Billy and a few more. I don't know you, though."

"Call us anything you want. Here's the problem: you guys got started early paying $20 an hour. We didn't care then because we weren't harvesting. Now, it's messing up the market."

"How so?" asked Pierce. I could feel his hackles rising from ten feet away. I was listening, but figured this was his job.

"Well Alexa here is getting $20 with you and her boyfriend is getting $15 with us. That's causing problems with them."

"You're doing couples counseling? That's nice. Alexa is working right now. Maybe you can schedule an appointment for them when they're off duty."

"Don't be a smartass."

"I'm not being a smartass. I'm paying Alexa to work right now.

She's lying to her boyfriend, by the way. She's getting $25 an hour as a premium trimmer."

"That's even worse. $25 an hour, for these . . . derelicts."

"Derelicts? I kind of like them. Different to be sure. Sometimes irresponsible, but we manage to negotiate suitable arrangements. It's not difficult. Step one might be to not call them derelicts."

"Now *you're* doing counseling. That's nice too."

"My counseling is free. It sounds like your counseling is going to cost Alexa $10 an hour."

"We can't get labor when you're paying $20. It's become a thing with all them. They'd rather not work than get $15. They think you've established the floor."

"OK. I don't know how *they* think but *they're* here working happily. It doesn't even make sense to talk about a *them*. There is no *them*. As far as I can determine, each individual does whatever the hell they want. The only collective behavior I've seen here is shitting in the woods when they're not supposed to. I'd find it refreshing if they have somehow banded together to actually make a *them*. I'd also be skeptical, surprised, and impressed. It's extremely unlikely."

"You need to lower the floor."

"Why don't you *raise* the floor? The way I hear it, all you growers are going to be making so much money you'll be lighting hundred-dollar bills to fire your spliffs. Why not spread some around?"

"How's your security around here? It looks wide open. Anyone with a box cutter could seriously mess up those vinyl hoophouse covers in about thirty seconds."

"We have twenty-four-hour security. Jake lives right over there. He's got an arsenal in his trailer. He might even have an AR–15, but I don't want to know. He said something the other day about hand grenades. What I do know is that he likes being an enforcer, since for most of his life, enforcement has gone the other way. He enjoys being on the right side for once. I wouldn't provoke him."

"That generator next to his trailer is pretty loud. And you're running twenty-four-hour shifts. Jake can't be everywhere at once. Those are two nice Munch Machines. Aren't they called a Motherbucker?"

"What did you call me?"

"I'm talking about the machines. I'd never call you a Mother *Bucker*. Don't they cost something like thirty grand apiece?"

"Actually they're $33,100. Maybe you should buy one instead of hacking your buds to powder with those machetes. Of course, they don't finance those machines. No talk, time payments, or courts of law. Too many snakes in the Hemp Space. Maybe you could sell three of those trucks and scrape enough green together and buy one of their starter models. They come with a manual. The manual has pictures."

"Maybe we'll just take one of yours. They look pretty portable, what with the big wheels and everything. I'm sure Alexa's boyfriend wouldn't mind doing a little moonlighting. Who the hell do you think you are anyway?"

"Who the hell are you? Some old hemp salt giving me the tried-and-true way? Maybe you've been in this biz fifteen minutes before me or fifteen minutes after, but there are no established people, enterprises, or norms here. We get to create them. Why not just be nice?"

"You're not being nice, playing word games, paying these hobos more than they're worth."

"I'm glad you noticed the word games. I wasn't sure you got that. You came here to talk to me. What do you have to say?"

"I'm saying we're gonna fuck you up if you don't drop to $15.

I'm saying we'll cut up your hoophouses, steal your equipment, and call the County and tell them you're running a commune or a trailer park or a goddam homeless shelter out here. Whatever you call this rotten setup, it's illegal in a dozen different ways. They'll shut you down in ten minutes."

I was enjoying this. I knew we were going to lose when I saw them drive up, but I didn't know exactly *how* we were going to lose. All points to Pierce on the verbal sparring and all points to the Neighborhood on the crux of the matter. With our fluid workforce, their divided loyalties, and the Neighborhood, there was no way we'd be able to protect the hoophouses, the machines, the product, or the workers. So much for the counterculture origins of the Hemp Space. This wasn't *Woodstock*; it was *Scarface*. I recognized a couple of the guys from the Grange meeting when I was trying to build bridges with hemp growers. They were probably the ones pocketing a roadie or two from the cooler for the drive home.

Pierce and I knew a shakedown when we saw one. We also knew when we were holding a pair of deuces against a full house. Pierce made the announcement at his Monday meeting, saying we'd honor the $20 an hour for the week, but after that, it was $15. Nobody left then, but the site became much quieter. My younger brother is a retired US Navy master chief petty officer. He once told me: "A bitching crew is a happy crew. When things go silent, that's the time to be very careful." Too true. Our crew worked in silence until Friday. On Saturday, about half our regular number showed up. But it didn't matter as far as the workflow went, because the empty spots were quickly filled in by latecomer trim-migrants; that they could squat on the farm was a big draw.

That visit changed the culture of our enterprise overnight. We'd been paying more to ensure we had workers, and being decent to them in other ways that weren't a hardship. Being forced to drop their pay wasn't an ethical conundrum; it was an existential threat. To our workers, we had simply joined the ranks of the exploiters, but it was obviously more complicated than that. The prime function of an enterprise is to survive. It needs to pay its bills, keep its employees, and have something left over for the owner. If tough decisions aren't made, the business fails, the bills go unpaid, the employees are laid off, and the owner goes bust. For most ethical small businesses, when money gets tight the first thing to go is the owner's salary, then it's lowering wages, then it's delaying supplier's bills. If none of those things work to turn things around, it's crunch time, and that's when true character emerges. Many wage-earners understand this and can even get on board with it if they see that senior staff is taking a hit too. It starts to get ugly when a company, like GM in 2008, flies their managers in a private jet to Washington, DC, to beg for a government bailout. That's beyond stupid.

There's also bankruptcy, as another often unethical release valve. Regardless of current fads, I'm an old fashioned guy and, well, bankruptcy courts are for wimps. If you have the character to start a business, then it's my unequivocal opinion that you need that same quality to shut it down in an orderly fashion. That means no lawyers, no courts, and no screwing of creditors. In most small business bankruptcies, the owner knows, long before the Culligan Man comes to take away the water cooler, that the business is going down. Still, many owners will continue their salaries and other perks while not paying suppliers, landlords, and utility companies, until any further choice of dispersal of remaining funds is taken away from them by a judge in a courtroom.

Starting a business entails enormous risk, and any potential business owner needs to assess that risk. That assessment should include paying off your obligations if things go sour. That's not the categorical imperative it used to be. I've watched this ethical floor recede significantly during my forty-five years in American business. There doesn't seem to be much stigma attached to becoming a bankrupt anymore. I think there ought to be. A bankrupt is required to stand before a judge and admit he can't cover the obligations he said he would. Bottom line: he's a deadbeat. All the people he didn't pay are lined up on the other side of the courtroom. It *ought* to be humiliating. I've had many businesses, and some of them didn't do so well, but I never faced a judge or left an unpaid bill in my wake. Sometimes I had to bust open my personal piggy bank to make things right, and that hurt, but I never doubted it was the right thing to do. Some folks, I won't call them businesspeople, think bankruptcy is a business tool. It's not. Bankruptcy, almost always, is the last refuge of the incompetent.

———

Happily, Pierce and I weren't anywhere near that point. We hadn't been pulling out any cash for ourselves, since there wasn't any, and Pierce was driving to work in his 1994 Toyota. What we did have, just delivered by our bookkeeping service, was a beautiful set of accurate monthly financial statements. We now knew the basic economics of post-harvest hemp processing.

Ten acres of outdoor hemp grown in Colorado for smokeable flower yielded about 15,000 plants weighing 45,000 lbs. The cost per acre was $12,000 from seed to harvest. Post-harvest costs went like this:

- Drying 45,000 pounds of hemp plants yielded about 20,000 pounds of dried material and cost $15 per pound for the resulting product, or $300,000.

- Bucking 20,000 pounds of dried hemp yielded about 10,000 pounds of untrimmed bud and cost $10 per pound, or $100,000.
- Trimming 10,000 pounds of bud yielded about 5,000 pounds of ready-to-sell smokeable flower and 5,000 pounds of biomass trim, and cost $20 per pound, for a total of another $100,000.

Let's add it all up. We have $120,000 in costs from seed to harvest, $300,000 for drying, $100,000 for bucking, and another $100,000 for trimming, for a grand total of $620,000, all in, on a ten-acre hemp farm. These are dauntingly big numbers, especially when you figure all these costs are up-front and there's no crop insurance either, so you're also at the mercy of an early freeze, pests, hail, theft, vandalism, and sabotage. Another way to look at it is to divide $620,000 by 10,000 pounds of product, so we know it costs us $62 per pound to bring hemp flower and trim to market. Obviously, we'll need to sell a pound of our product for more than $62.

Why on earth did more than 2,500 farmers in Colorado sign up for this? One reason was that hardly anyone knew the real costs beforehand. The CDA sure didn't. The other reason was that, on one level, the costs didn't matter if hemp flower was selling for $350 a pound. The weedwhackers 5,000 pounds of flower and 5,000 pounds of biomass would have sold for over $2 million. Subtract $620,000 in expenses and there's a net profit of about $1.5 million, or $150,000 an acre.

That huge projected profit figure was the gas poured onto the fire that fueled the Colorado hemp boom. In contrast, corn *might* net $250 per acre, usually less.

Pierce and I were thrilled to have finally figured all this out.

Those numbers would have been very useful a year earlier to several thousand hemp farmers. Still, solving the accounting mystery didn't solve our current banking problem.

The day we couldn't pay our crew because the bank closed us down wasn't a catastrophe, but it was embarrassing. I don't like to be embarrassed as a business owner. It doesn't matter to me if it's trimmigrants or fancy bankers, my word is my bond, and the status of the recipient is irrelevant to that standard.

We needed another bank, fast. Most of the hemp folks in Colorado used Wells Fargo because they were legendary for opening business accounts without asking questions. This came from the company policy of linking a local bank manager's compensation with the number of new accounts opened. There was a massive scandal starting in 2016 when regulators discovered that Wells Fargo managers were creating millions of phantom accounts to boost their pay. As has been widely reported, the bank paid $2.7 billion in fines for the practice and pledged to mend its ways.

When I walked into the local Wells Fargo branch, I was ready to tell the story about moving services, but it never came up and I soon had an account. At least it was a *real* account, which might be viewed as some progress in changing the culture at Wells Fargo, but that was the regulator's problem, not mine.

I was glad to have another bank, but I was still uneasy. At any moment a banker might start asking questions about all those cash withdrawals and wonder if I was connected in any way to hemp.

If I thought I had problems, the people in the legal marijuana business in Colorado were in a crisis. If they were honest about their business, they couldn't find *any* bank, not even Wells Fargo, to handle their accounts. They couldn't find a credit card processor either, or any place to deposit checks. One had a processor in Portugal; I discovered this when I bought some CBD product online and saw on the website that the charge would appear from a bank in Lisbon.

There were a couple of credit unions in Colorado that handled hemp and marijuana accounts, but I couldn't find one without a two-year waiting list. There were also whispers that some regular banks handled these accounts, but if they were or are, they're not advertising. Consequently, the entire marijuana industry operated on cash. Among many issues, this meant that legal marijuana dispensaries were an obvious target for burglary, and, in fact, burglaries were commonplace.

On Tax Day in Denver, when businesses have to pay their sales and excise taxes, it was said there was a line of Brink's trucks a mile long at the Colorado Department of Revenue, bringing all that cash from the dispensaries to the state treasury.

Naturally, the industry figured out workarounds. A common one was that legal marijuana dispensaries would deposit their funds with a business consultant who would make the deposits as consulting fees. This was clunky and transparent.

Even worse for the legal marijuana dispensaries was IRS rule 280E, which disallowed normal business deductions. The biggest expense, cost of goods sold, is so murky as to be undefinable, but other expenses like salaries, rent, utilities, insurance, advertising, marketing, repairs/maintenance, and payments to contractors were definitely *not* deductible. Legal marijuana dispensaries had to pay income taxes on something very close to their gross annual sales. I wouldn't call that merely inconvenient; I'd call it a tax shakedown on a grand scale. One legal marijuana producer told me he got into the Hemp Space largely to mitigate 280E. While his hemp sales were a fraction of his dispensary sales, he would be able to deduct hemp expenses the way a normal business could. His company was profitable, but even with $3 million in sales, it couldn't sustain both him and his partner on a salary. He ended up going back to his old job in Big Pharma. That's entirely due to 280E, and one more negative effect of our government's absurd War on Drugs.

While most of these problems were confined to legal marijuana businesses, hemp enterprises were often tarred with the same brush, and I still had a banking problem to solve. I wasn't confident I'd be able to keep my account at Wells Fargo. I needed a bank where I could come clean about the business I was in and where they wouldn't get spooked by large cash transactions. That's when I found Bank of the West. Bank of the West was a subsidiary of BNP Paribas, a French company, and they had decided to open accounts in the Hemp Space.

This was revolutionary and I'll be forever grateful to them. Bank of the West understood that for hemp to become the billion-dollar business it might evolve into, business owners needed a bank to handle the transactions, the loans, the credit instruments, the card processing, indeed the entire banking infrastructure any industry requires. Nobody else was doing it but them and a few credit unions. The compliance costs were enormous, and it was a big risk for the bank in other ways. One infraction from a rogue or careless hemp account could subject them to millions of dollars in fines. They needed risk specialists, all making six-figure salaries, monitoring every single account, every day, every transaction.

When I went to the local branch and told them I wanted to open a hemp account, they said there was a special department for that. They gave me the business card for the hemp specialist at their Littleton branch. I sent her an email and got one back in a couple of hours. She scheduled a phone call and we talked for a long time. She didn't beat around the bush, and I had the immediate impression that here was a serious person, with a serious bank behind her looking for real business. She grilled me about our hemp processing business, my business experience, our projected revenue, our expenses, who were we working with, and where we were located.

"This all sounds good," she said after nearly an hour on the phone, "but I have to verify everything. I can come out tomorrow for a site visit."

"Site visit?"

"Site visit. I check out all my potential clients, in person. Does tomorrow work?" I got the distinct impression that if tomorrow didn't work, our relationship would never get started.

"Tomorrow's fine."

She showed up the next day in banker's clothing and heels, which was kind of awkward on a hemp farm. Our facility was going full-bore and she checked out the hoophouses, our equipment, saw all the workers, and examined our product. She asked to see our Certificates of Analysis (COA), and we chatted in general about the Hemp Space in Colorado. She knew everyone worth knowing and told us she'd signed up over two hundred hemp accounts in just a few months and had essentially invented her job at Bank of the West. At the end of the visit, she said she'd give the higher-ups a positive recommendation, but it could take up to sixty days to get all the paperwork through compliance. A couple of weeks later, she called to tell us we were approved and ready for a deposit. We went over the fee structure and I was prepared to get raked over the coals, but the fees were standard stuff.

In addition to that, she was accessible all the time and gave sensible advice. "Never deliver product without being paid by either a wire transfer, certified check, or cash. You're an established hemp account here now and we know a lot of business is done in cash. Make sure each cash deposit has an invoice attached and you'll be fine. Did I say don't hand over product without getting paid? It's worth saying twice, three times."

Now that's twenty-first-century banking. I'll be banking at Bank of the West until that final check clears at the funeral parlor for my cremation.

What I've heard on the street since then is that the really big banks make "exceptions" for large hemp accounts. While Bank of the West was incubating hemp businesses, as soon as they got big, the majors would poach them away with all sorts of goodies.

It's a jungle out there. Bankers are the lions.

Chapter 9
PAYDAY

I'm a "work hard play hard" kind of guy, and Pierce and I needed a break. I'll relent a millimeter here and allow that taking a little break is fine in the early startup phase provided the time off is related to your business. I'm aware this implacable focus can be hard on relationships, but it's the price to pay if you want to succeed in business for yourself. You don't get to punch out. That precept left only one candidate for a little R & R: we'd decamp for Vegas and check out the massive MJBIZ convention. MJBIZ had started as an annual gathering for the legal marijuana business, but after the Farm Bill passed, it expanded into the Hemp Space. Pierce and I both knew we were lacking essential information about what the hell we were doing and figured hanging at the convention might fill in some of our gaps. We were both excited to get away from the farm, even if it was only two days.

The convention started at 9 a.m., exceedingly early for the cannabis crowd, but Pierce and I got there at 8 anyway. I didn't want to be late or not have enough time to do all the booths or get hung up in a long line. I'd done twenty years of New York fashion shows at both the Piers and the Javits Center. Every year I walked every aisle and looked into every booth. If you want to find the golden nugget, you have to do it that way. I explained my philosophy to Pierce, and he agreed. He's an agreeable guy and had never been to a trade show before, so he let me lead. I know my trade show method is unconventional, but most of my enterprises have outlasted the critics.

We waited outside, people-watching and wondering how all these folks might have made a living before hemp. Here at Hemp Central Station, it was even easier to pick out the budtenders from the narcotourists. They let us inside at 8:30 to get coffee in the atrium. If I was wondering how this would go with Pierce, I shouldn't have. At the coffee station he asked the heavyset guy next to him if he wanted cream and sugar. Then he beamed his six-foot-four-inch smile at him, put out his hand, and said, "I'm Pierce. I'm a hemp processor. What's your gig?" It's a hard opening to resist from Pierce, and well, this *was* a trade show. The guy responded warmly, "I'm Malouf. Nice to meet you. I'm *the* hemp guy in LA. I had some extra time, and I like Vegas, so I thought I'd check things out. I'll take the cream, no sugar. I'm watching my waistline." Pierce handed over the creamer. "We're just a couple of farmers from Colorado. We're not a big-time guy like you. Let's exchange business cards." Boom. Pierce had his first contact.

Over the next two days we walked the show, stopping at booths and chatting with salespeople. The biggest vendor booths were the extraction supply companies. They came from Germany, Taiwan, the USA, and China, with lavish displays of 25-foot-high stainless steel chambers connected to labyrinthine systems of pipe. Those booths looked like oil refineries in miniature, which I guess they were. Next biggest were the merchandising companies, which promised to turn your extracted oil into a slickly packaged consumer product. At the low end were the hemp machinery companies, which turned plants into smokeable flower. Munch Machine, Green Broz, Centurion, and Triminator were there, but that niche was a small market for the show in general even though it was the main market for Pierce and me.

Down one aisle were several booths selling ATM machines. We stopped at one, staffed by a man in a cowboy hat, and I asked, "You mean an individual can own an ATM?"

"Of course," he said, eyeing me like the rube I was. "There are way more ATMs in convenience stores and gas stations than at banks. These little retailers *own* their machines, man. You fill it with money, take the fee, and dump out the cash. The transaction is immediately charged to the customer's card, and you get your money back that night, plus the fee, into your bank account from the processor. It's just like a retailer merchant agreement. We don't discriminate. Dope dealers can buy our machines."

"We're not dope dealers. What's the fee on those machines to the cardholder?"

"Whatever you want. Some states have limits but it's a gray area. Every smart dispensary has an ATM. It's another profit center. The narcotourists come to Colorado from Kansas, Nebraska, New Jersey"—he made a deprecating motion toward himself, indicating his shirt, with the top four buttons open, a hirsute upper chest, and gold crucifix. "They don't know you can't use a credit card at these places when they go in. They want their buds, dude. They find out they can't pay with a card, and they think they're screwed, but they're not. The nice budtender just smiles and says, 'No problem, we have an ATM right over there.' The dispensary can charge 5% or more. When people want their weed, they want their weed, especially when they're on vacation. Our starter model is $2,500. How many do you want?"

"I didn't say we wanted any. I just asked a question."

"We also offer cash stocking and maintenance services. Set up an account with us, we'll keep the machine full of money and maintain it. We have twenty-four-hour service crews on call nationwide. We'll do that for a 1% monthly total transaction value, or we can bill you a flat monthly rate. It all depends on your volume. Your customer thinks it's a convenience for them, but it's really a profit machine for *you*. Our rates are very competitive and we're a one-stop shop. Buy our machine and we become your very dependable partner. How many machines did you say you wanted?" He grabbed his clipboard to write up our order.

"Slow down. We're just walking the show and taking notes."

"Sure." He turned away to greet the group standing next to us. "Howdy folks." He tipped his absurd hat and grabbed his belt buckle. "Y'all looking for some extra profits?"

Grabbed his belt buckle? What the hell was that? Something he saw in a John Wayne movie when he was a kid at the Asbury Park drive-in? *Y'all*? We don't say "y'all" in Colorado and we certainly don't grab our belt buckles as a greeting ritual.

What a country! You can own your own ATM! Subsequent research revealed that everything this absurdly fast-talking, hard-working culture chameleon said was true. On-site ATMs *do* prevent customers from walking out empty-handed. It's what we old retailers call "saving the sale," and one that adds solid profit into the mix.

While privately held ATMs may have solved the point-of-sale problem for dispensaries, it didn't solve their cash problem. Dispensaries were stockpiling huge amounts of cash with no bank to put it in. Another big aisle at the convention featured safe manufacturers like Chubb and money wagon companies like Brink's and Dunbar. Clearly, the hemp tide was lifting other boats, and lots of these boats, like Chubb, were in the Fortune 500. The Brink's booth was staffed by two middle-aged white men in very nice suits (the only suits I saw that day) and a third guy dressed as a Brink's driver complete with muscles, massive frame, holster, gun, and attitude. No doubt this trio would have been a highly successful team at an American Banking Association convention in Branson, Missouri, but here at MJBIZ they looked like the three stooges. I'm sure they could feel it too. Most of the people walking by their booth probably looked less like potential customers than the kind of threat their regular clients hired Brink's to protect them from.

We stopped at another booth and talked to the glove maven. I'd never thought a lot about gloves, but on the hemp farm, our trimmigrants were going through several hundred pairs of disposable gloves a day. We were buying them at Home Depot and spending a small fortune. The guy in this booth lived and breathed gloves.

"Latex is so twentieth-century. Lots of people are allergic to latex. Nitrile is the only way to go. Stronger, no chemical transference, puncture-resistant. Our five-mil gloves are used in hospitals all over the world. This is a weird show for us. We usually work with hospital administrators and doctors, not dope dealers."

"We're not dope dealers. We're hemp processors."

"Sorry. I meant no offense. I don't really care what you do. This show isn't our core business. I don't even know why they assigned me to this. I care about gloves, and I know gloves. If you've got a risk of getting a bunch of toxic crap on your hands, we've got the affordable solution."

"Hemp isn't toxic, it's just sticky."

"Who knows from toxic? I don't. You don't either. Our nitrile gloves are slightly more expensive, I'll admit, but you won't be getting any lawsuits from your staff because of transmissions of bad stuff."

"I very much doubt our trimmigrants will be filing lawsuits."

"Trimmigrants?"

"The people who process hemp plants. They're not exactly an organized group."

"That's what everyone says, right before the class action shitstorm."

"We appreciate your time."

"Our gloves are made in the USA, too. Maybe that doesn't mean anything to you, but it means a lot to us."

"We'll take a business card." We left the booth and he followed us a little way down the aisle shoving some free samples into our hands.

"Did I tell you our gloves are waterproof?"

God, I do love trade shows.

We flew back to Denver on the Monday. As it happened, we ended up ordering 10,000 pairs of blue nitrile gloves from the glove maven and sold Malouf 20 pounds of hemp flower. Alas, Malouf never received his shipment because it was snagged by FedEx as suspected marijuana and we had to return his money.

———

Since our deal with the weedwhackers didn't have a set price for services, we had agreed to provide them with all of our financials and negotiate an invoice. When it was totaled up, we had spent over $350,000 in ninety days for labor and equipment to prepare their crop for market. It was time to get paid.

In putting our invoice together, Pierce and I figured it three different ways.

The first was to get information on what other post-harvesters were charging. Pierce worked the phones and prepared a spreadsheet detailing all the companies in the US we could find along with their pricing schedules. According to that calculation, the weedwhacker bill should have been about $580,000. That's a profit margin I was used to from my years operating retail stores, but I thought it was a bit high. We'd received a lot of help from the weedwhackers, the hoophouses were on their farm without rent, and they'd been generous with lending us their tractor. Even though they expected to gross almost $2 million, that wasn't really any of our business. We wanted a decent return but didn't want to gouge anybody, regardless of their ultimate profits. We adjusted the price down 20% in recognition of their contribution, for a total of $464,000.

Our second method was to total up the expenses and attach a reasonable profit margin. The expenses came to about $350,000, which with a 35% margin of $122,500 gave a total of $472,500.

The last method was to simply charge them $40 per pound for drying, bucking, and trimming on their 11,944 pounds of product. That came to $477,760.

This brought us a lot of comfort, since all three methods arrived at a remarkably similar number that could be readily explained and, if necessary, defended.

We were due to meet early in December at the temporary office we'd rented next to the farm. Pierce had evolved from construction manager to processing manager to hemp salesman. He was using the office, which ironically was above a legal marijuana dispensary, as his headquarters to find buyers for the weedwhacker flower. This wasn't panning out particularly well for us, nor were the sales efforts of the weedwhackers themselves. Buyers weren't exactly sprouting, and all those visitors to the farm in July were nowhere to be found. The dearth of sales wasn't due to anyone's lack of effort. It was simply that all the boom–bust dynamics had converged in Colorado that autumn.

The first torpedo to strike the hull came from the USDA and their Interim Final Rule. Under heavy pressure from the DEA, the USDA unilaterally altered their definition of hot hemp. Even though the Rule wouldn't go into effect until the following year, it confused everybody. A lot of the hemp in Colorado was hot by the new standard, which meant that shipping hemp to other states might be viewed as marijuana dealing. Very few hemp buyers understood the implications of the new USDA rule, so they decided to sit this one out. I've done my share of cold-call sales and the ideal opening pitch is not, "Hi. What I'm selling isn't illegal, regardless of what you might have heard."

The next torpedo was the sheer volume of hemp being harvested. Colorado led the country with over 80,000 acres, but Oregon, California, Kentucky, and North Carolina were close behind. Oversupply caused the price to crash, and the $350 per pound for hemp flower the previous year was suddenly a fond but distant memory.

An artillery salvo came in from the extractors. While there was a glut of folks ready to turn your crop into oil or isolate, they'd spent all their capital building labs. Extractors weren't buying hemp biomass for cash anymore. They were only offering what they called tolling agreements, which meant they'd take your crop, process it, and give you a percentage of the oil or isolate back in payment. This didn't work for the farmers, who were out of cash too. They didn't need CBD; they needed the mortgage payment. A nasty by-product of the extractor glut was an oversupply of oil and isolate, so those prices crashed too.

The final straw that turned the boom into a bust was the lack of a centralized marketplace where buyers and sellers could unite and let a new floor price reset itself. Even a low price would have been better than no price. Each farmer had to find his own buyer, ergo our office next to the farm, with Pierce and a weed-whacker working the phones. The sad and naked truth was that nobody in Colorado, or anywhere else, could be found who'd pay cold cash for biomass or smokeable flower at any price. There *was* no marketplace.

Naturally, this put the wind up the weedwhackers. Their dream of $2 million had sunk beneath the waves and they were in a lifeboat taking on water. They weren't in a panic just yet. They believed that some sort of floor price would be established, and they'd just have to wait it out. In the meantime, they told us, it was important to store the flower properly. Processed hemp flower needs to be stored at 60 degrees Fahrenheit and 60% humidity to prevent deterioration of the CBD content. Without those conditions, it would also be susceptible to mold, mildew, and a degraded nose and color.

They needed a truly climate-controlled facility, of which there were exactly none in Colorado. Indoor so-called climate-controlled mini storage facilities are everywhere, but they're only temperature-controlled. None of them have *humidity* control. Humid, hot, and dark are ideal conditions for mold and mildew. Lots of hemp growers, not knowing this, planned to use these mini-storage places; but, just like the banks, indoor storage companies wouldn't take hemp clients. They had a better reason. A ten-by-ten storage unit filled with hemp, no matter how well packaged it was, would have the whole facility smelling like a Phish concert in twenty-four hours.

This opened up another exciting business opportunity and one I could actually use my farm for: climate-controlled hemp storage. I had a big empty barn on the property just sitting there. Call me a chump or a genius, but I doubled down and had a concrete floor poured, bought an insulated overhead door, painted the whole space in flat white, and had Manuel, bless his heart, install a humidity and heat control system. Two weeks and $20,000 later, we had Colorado's only completely climate-controlled hemp storage facility. The weedwhackers didn't immediately put their hemp in there, though. They were still hoping the market would shift and they'd sell their stuff quickly.

This was the dismal business environment when we held our first meeting about getting paid. We presented a bill for $460,000 with the three financial scenarios supporting the numbers and gave them the statements prepared by our bookkeeper. It got very quiet. I don't know what the weedwhackers were expecting; they'd been there from day one, watching the hoophouses being built, seeing the equipment come in, and working alongside our trimmigrant army. Any back-of-the-envelope calculation would have come in at medium six figures. I suspect their surprise at our bill had more to do with them continually lowering their expectations about how much they might sell their crop for than what it might have cost to process. Our view was that their expected profits— whether $2 million or less than that—was none of our business. We'd provided the services they had asked for.

After a very long silence, one of them said that this was way out of their expected range. "What about other farmers?" one of them asked. "You were supposed to get a bunch of other hemp to spread the costs. You guys failed and now we're supposed to pay for that?"

Pierce jumped in on that one: "We didn't fail. The timing didn't work because the plants took longer to dry and process than you estimated. We guaranteed you guys would get first dibs. You got first dibs. We brought in Billy's stuff, and you got all upset because you thought it would affect your drying time. It didn't. We all thought it made sense a few months ago, when none of us knew anything, that we could keep the hoophouses churning plants from other farms. We all know now it doesn't work that way, and we now know why. You needed all the hoophouses all the time for the processing and you got them. You had no problem with that at the time, and we didn't either. Now, it seems you do."

"So, your business plan was all wrong. That's not our problem."

"Our business plan wasn't all wrong. We were hired to execute *your* plan. We executed your plan, including major unexpected equipment purchases, higher labor costs, and extra time for drying. The work and the equipment costs are what they are. You provided us with estimates of workflow, machinery, and drying time that didn't come even close to fitting the reality. We're not blaming anybody. We were all operating in uncharted waters. We didn't waste any money. You were there. You know we ran a tight ship. You have the financials in front of you. There were variables that needed adjusting in real time. We did that, and we did that under your supervision, and with your support. Your crop took more time and resources than you thought and that prevented us from taking on more clients. It's still not a problem, so let's not make it one.

"But if you do want to talk about business plans that went wrong, then your expectation of $350 per pound was wrong. We don't see that as our problem. We see that as *your* problem. We did the work, supervised by you. You were happy, as I recall, with the finished product we delivered. Now it's time to pay up."

"These prices for processing on this sheet are bogus. Where did you get these numbers?"

Pierce was still at the helm. "I called every processor I could find. You want to check them out, go ahead. We can make the calls together. I've got all the contacts."

"Good idea. It can't cost that much."

Pierce was supremely affronted. He hadn't had a day off since August 28, and he had been successfully navigating the weed-whackers' changing needs, trimmigrants, irate neighbors, labor issues, and the CDA. Six feet four inches of serious Irish grievance can be very intimidating. I let Pierce have at it up to a point, but the tension in the room was rising. I wasn't pleased either, but I was more concerned with getting the money we were owed than letting off steam. I dropped in as the good cop:

"Look, guys, we've worked really well together for several months. There's no cause here for acrimony. If you don't like the bill, then take some time to go over it. We'll be happy to discuss adjustments."

The meeting ended on that note, but the air in that office was arctic.

We put the same scenario together for Billy Held and he didn't like his bill either. We went over the statements together and he explained how he could have done every line item cheaper. I've no doubt that was true. We reminded him that he had called us the day before the big freeze and was facing the total loss of his crop. We also reminded him that we told him at the time he wouldn't like our fee. Billy acknowledged those points and we quickly agreed on an invoice amount and payment terms. Billy groaned a lot, but he eventually paid us in full—and we're still friendly.

We met again with the weedwhackers in January after Pierce and one of them had gotten together and called the other process-ing companies. Pierce's numbers checked out, but that didn't change anything.

The weedwhackers might have thrown us a bone with a check for a hundred grand or so to let some air out of the tension balloon, but they didn't. Pierce and I offered several different scenarios where the weedwhackers could keep the hoophouses and the equipment and just pay us for labor plus a small profit. This would get us our money back and leave them with the infrastructure to continue. No dice. It became clear to us that the weedwhackers wanted to treat us as if we'd been partners, and share the loss. There had been no talk about partnership when hemp was $350 per pound. That might have been fine back then, but being ex post facto partners in only their liabilities was a nonstarter. We were their vendor, not their partner. After that meeting, one of the weedwhackers called me up and asked me:

"How do you expect to get paid when we can't sell our hemp?"

I was starting to get my own Irish up. "Is that what you tell T-Mobile? Is that what you tell the utility company, your seed supplier, your irrigation consultant? 'Aww gee, we didn't make our sales numbers, the dog ate our spreadsheet, there was too much rain, or not enough rain, or we couldn't find labor or paid too many laborers,' or whatever. Those are called excuses and that's how they're viewed by service providers who did their job. That's what we are. We're your post-harvest processor. We're no different than all those folks just mentioned, all of whom got paid. You, as a businessman, are supposed to be capitalized well enough to cover your obligations. Win or lose, you're supposed to pay your bills."

"You're being unreasonable. Your bill is too high, and, in a way, it doesn't matter what the bill is. We can't pay it. Even a smaller one. We can't pay *any* of your bill until we move some product."

"We're not actually asking for payment right now. We've been asking for an agreement on what the invoice amount should be. This goes way back to us at the coffee shop in August. We agreed we'd negotiate an amount. You guys just saying 'no' isn't a negotiation."

"It all depends on what we sell the product for."

"We know you see it that way. We don't. We're not your part-ner. You keep telling us our number is too high, but we've backed up our number three different ways with data. The question isn't what you're going to sell your product for but whether our number is a fair number."

Round and round it went. In all our discussions, we'd offered generous terms regarding when the payment would be made. We did this to give them time to sell their flower. We weren't pressing them for payment, nor were we particularly firm on the $460,000. The only point we were pressing hard on was an invoice amount we could agree on. We never got one. All we ever got was an admission that they couldn't pay any amount without selling some product.

Wouldn't and *couldn't* are interesting business terms. When the weedwhackers said they couldn't pay, what they really meant was that they wouldn't.

This brings up an interesting point between legality and eth-ics in business. It's perfectly legal to set up an LLC with no assets, and it's perfectly legal for that LLC to renege on its obligations when the revenue stream turns sour. The ethics of the matter are not the same.

The flip side of the hymn to business startups I sang back when I was laying out the hoophouses is that it's no less important to dismantle an enterprise that doesn't work out in a businesslike fashion. There's no music to that dance at all. Operating a business with no future is not pleasant, but there are still important aes-thetic and ethical reasons to close it down properly.

Through the winter and spring, we met with the weedwhack-ers at various times. Pierce and I brought several more options to the table, but we weren't progressing. The hemp flower market wasn't improving much either, though the weedwhackers were selling product here and there and keeping the money.

Our final meeting was in April. It had been eight months and we still hadn't seen a dollar or agreed on an invoice amount. We'd given them seven different ways to pay, always asking for a number they could live with, but it never came.

In the middle of all this, their crop had been transferred to a weedwhacker barn with no humidity or temperature control and had started to dry out. One day, a second weedwhacker asked if he could bring some product over to our climate-controlled barn to rehydrate for a customer. I said sure, so in mid-April he brought a truckload over in a U-Haul and the two of us had a quiet chat with nobody else there.

"Look," he said, "we want to pay, but the amount is too much."

"Give us a number."

"My partners aren't willing to do that. It depends on what they get from hemp sales."

"That's the central issue. You think the price of hemp is somehow related to our invoice amount and we don't. We're willing to come down from 460K but if we do, you'll have to provide some kind of security for payment."

"What kind of security?"

"Something ironclad. Like a second mortgage on a farm property, vehicles, a personal guarantee. We've been arguing for months. If we're going to cave on our invoice, which we've always been prepared to a certain extent to do, then we need to be sure we'll get something."

"I'll talk to the partners."

The next day, a different weedwhacker called Pierce in a rage. According to Pierce, he wasn't going to talk to me ever again, he was outraged that I'd supposedly turn his family out onto the streets. This was nonsense; he wasn't getting turned out, he was being asked to pay his bills.

Pierce endured two days of vitriolic tantrums and then we received an eviction letter from him saying that the hoophouses needed to be removed from the weedwhacker farm by April 30. That was an escalation. That same day, the other weedwhacker, apparently unaware of his partner's diatribes or the eviction notice, asked Pierce if he could bring *all* the hemp to our barn for rehydration. Pierce said sure, and everything was brought over to our climate-controlled barn.

Here we were, in a dispute about payment, and they placed their entire inventory in our hands. And that's when I called in the lawyers. We'd had enough, and like everyone who's had enough, we wanted more. In forty-five years of business, I had never sued anyone or been sued. Some folks enjoy conflict like that, but I'm not one of them. I rooted around my contacts for a referral to a bulldog litigation firm.

In our first consultation with the litigator, an affable and blunt gentleman we'll call Biff, he asked us to sketch out the details of our complaint. We gave him the bones and Biff indicated that it was probable they'd created an empty LLC with no assets and, even if we won at trial, we'd get nothing but his legal bills.

I pointed out that they had brought all their hemp the day before to store in our climate-controlled barn. This was a fact that Biff couldn't quite bring himself to believe. His thinking was that nobody would hand over merchandise that hadn't been paid for in the middle of a trade dispute. We convinced him eventually, but his initial thought was that we'd stolen it. It took a little time for Biff to believe we were legitimate, truthful, and liquid. Those litigators live and breathe skepticism and generally reserve more of it for their potential clients than their adversaries. I don't blame them.

Our guy kept it simple. This was breach of contract and unjust enrichment. Basic business law. It had nothing to do with hemp, though he did say that the Hemp Space looked like fat city going forward for lawyers.

He recommended we file the two complaints the next day and asked for a $10,000 retainer. That would get us through writing up the complaints, filing the liens, and serving the papers. After that, it would be more money to respond to their response. If we went all the way to trial, we'd be in for well over a hundred grand.

This was a different kind of law than I'd ever experienced. I'd paid lawyers for decades on lease agreements, forming corporations, defining partnerships, estate planning, and real estate. All those were about making or conserving money. Litigation is trying to get money owed or returned from people who don't want to hand it over. It's a very different dynamic, and this law firm was very careful with respect to invoicing. They *never* got behindhand on money, no doubt having bitter experience in that regard.

So we sued the weedwhackers the next day for $485,000, locked the barn, closed the gate on our farm, installed a video camera, and put up No Trespassing signs. The Rubicon had been crossed. Biff's complaint was a masterful document. Thirty-nine pages of malfeasance, bad intentions, and hints of criminal activity. Ten days later, right on the deadline, we received the weedwhacker reply. Twenty or so pages of obfuscating denial. Biff was thrilled, and maybe a little disappointed, to see such weak opposition. He was really enjoying this. I was not. Biff wanted to push for a jury trial as soon as possible. His view was that jurors don't like deadbeats and the weedwhacker attorney knew that too. His real motive was to get the weedwhackers to settle. Essentially the same thing we'd been trying to get them to do.

And that's what we got. A threadbare settlement offer from the weedwhacker attorney. Biff sent the whole email thread, and I was struck by the collegial tone between the two attorneys. It was all politeness and deference with a lot of Respectfully Yours, and Please Be So Kind to Respond verbiage. Biff called and recommended we reject since he thought they'd be back with a better one. We rejected.

Another settlement offer came and went. Then another. Each one had slightly better terms, but nothing close to the $485,000 we were suing for. Biff explained that we were suing the LLC and had no idea as to the assets there. Probably none. They had told Pierce in one of their tantrums that it was an empty shell.

After three offers Biff figured there weren't going to be any more. He said it was time for us to make a counter-offer and assume there would be no cash in this deal. He recommended we get as much product as possible and call the whole thing off. He also said that what he'd really like would be to obliterate them in a courtroom but knew we wouldn't spend $100,000 in fees to just please him and most likely end up with oongots, as they say in Naples.

So that's what happened. I can't discuss the settlement, though any passer-by can see that the hoophouses are still on their farm but cannot see how much smokeable flower remained in our barn.

With the lawsuit finished, Pierce and I decided we were also finished with post-harvest processing as some sort of business. It was now late June and we'd been in the Hemp Space for exactly one year with nothing much to show for it but a quantity of hemp flower and biomass in our nice climate-controlled barn. If this was last year, we could have sold it off to recoup our expenses, but this wasn't last year. Biomass was selling for two bucks instead of $80, and flower was selling for $50, maybe, instead of $350. I also had $150,000 worth of equipment to sell off. I'd spent over

$350,000 to process the weedwhacker hemp, but that was back at the end of October. We'd processed for Billy Held and another small farmer and that kept the business going. This was almost a year later. If we continued to September, I'd be in for $500,000 plus the machinery.

It was time to cut our losses and liquidate assets in a down market.

PART III
RISKY BUSINESS

Chapter 10
MIDDLEMEN

To be clear, Pierce and I weren't throwing in the towel on the whole Hemp Space. Sure, we were done with the processing part. But even if everything had panned out according to plan, we knew we'd have to create more revenue to make this venture a success. We weren't going to flourish on a seventy-five-day autumn harvest business with three hoophouses located on someone else's farm.

We had learned the hard lesson that's been learned by every farmer since that first caveman decided to toss some seeds into the ground rather than eat them: product producers don't usually end up with the spoils. I should have known this from my cashmere days. It wasn't the goat herder in Mongolia who was flying to New York fashion week in a chartered airplane. It was me, the middleman.

The hemp farmers had overplanted and there was too much product out there, which caused the price to crash. That's Economics 101. Why I thought hemp would be different than trapping beavers, or drilling oil, or mining gold was my blunder, and I'll own it. In slight mitigation I will mention that I'd been fed a bunch of mythic drivel about family farmers, probably from the same folks that deify Western ranchers, from childhood. Also, the well-meaning cheerleaders down at the Colorado Department of Agriculture played no meager part. The bureaucrats knew doodley-squat about seed-to-harvest costs, post-harvest processing costs, or the hemp marketplace, yet they encouraged everyone to pile into hemp.

It wasn't all bad news, though. The CBD consumer market was still booming and switching gears quickly is part of being in an early-stage industry, or in this case, space. Pierce and I had made our bones as a flexible team. We were also optimistic, and those are two requirements for success. We decided to re-explore brokering, crowded as it was. Trading textiles had been a lot more crowded than the Hemp Space, and I'd managed to make a success of that. Besides, we had two things most brokers didn't, which were flower and biomass in our possession, properly stored, and ready for sale. There were at least a hundred hemp brokerages just in Denver, and they were all looking for salespeople. Pierce came up with the idea of getting a job with one of those outfits to learn the trade.

This wasn't a huge leap because Pierce's previous work experience had all been in sales. He'd done everything: front end in restaurants, retail in a shopping mall, canvassing folks on Sixteenth Street in Denver, and cold-calling VRBO owners selling service contracts. He'd been on a steady upward march and was very successful in his last sales job before he jumped ship to sail with me across this uncharted ocean of hemp.

For Pierce, landing a job in hemp sales wasn't difficult given his résumé and manner, plus the fact that not a single one of those jobs paid a salary. Any brokerage would happily give you a cubicle in some bland office building and tell you to go for it. They'd pay a commission on any sales you generated and if you generated no sales, you made no money. Given that little wrinkle, we agreed that I'd continue his salary while he learned the ropes. It was an investment. Things were fine between Pierce and me. Better than fine. Other than not getting paid by the weedwhackers, we really enjoyed working together and we didn't think it would take too long to figure out if there was any money in brokering.

Pierce took a job with ADM Labs, which was not connected with ADM, the Fortune 500 commodity giant from Chicago, nor was it a lab. It was named for the initials of the founder, who's from Dubai. It's unclear if he knew that those initials invoked fear, loathing, and respect in anyone dealing in agricultural commodities.

I had initially contacted ADM Labs a year earlier because I thought it *was* related to the big ADM. I'd already had my fill of shady extractors and consultants and figured that while the real ADM might be a colossus, and a vortex for those who liked to criticize Big Ag, it was probably a colossus that paid its bills, which was a damn sight more than the New Economy capitalists in the Hemp Space seemed to be doing.

My first contact at ADM Labs had been with Nico Anthony, the managing director. Back then I was looking for a company that would give us a contract for the hemp I was planning to grow. Nico met with me in the basement of their four-story office building in Denver. The basement was bursting with super-sacks full of hemp. (A super-sack is a woven polypropylene bag that holds about 500 pounds of hemp.) Nico explained to me that organic Boulder County hemp was a high-demand product, that they'd likely buy my crop, but they weren't ready just then to write a contract or settle on any kind of pricing. "Things are too fluid," he said. That was honest of him and too true.

So, a year later, I introduced Pierce to Nico and Pierce got his desk on the ADM Labs trading floor. It looked impressive. There were a dozen or so cubicles in a large room and they were all occupied by busy-looking twenty- or thirty-somethings. Just like the budtenders, hemp salesmen were a post-racial but not post-gender group. It was all guys, with the same man buns, tats, or even more dramatic manifestations of latter-day individuality like face piercings. None of this matters to me in the least except to say that a blond Viking hemp trader looks weird in dreadlocks while a Jamaican hemp trader doesn't.

Pierce's new job entailed cold-calling CBD stores, extractors, people he'd met, and various companies he'd found to sell them some flower, oil, isolate, or any other hemp products ADM Labs sold, such as CBD-infused honey. He'd been upfront with Nico that he was winding down the post-harvest business with me and he'd be splitting his time. Nico didn't mind. Everyone there was splitting their time and had several plates spinning with other gigs, so Pierce fit right in, except for his office hours, which were nine to five. That immediately made him an eccentric. Hemp sales was not a morning business. It was barely an afternoon business. It was actually not a business at all. It was rolling dice with a dollop of hope tossed in. You didn't really find buyers. Buyers found you, if you were lucky, and, well, you might make some luck by starting early and working the phones.

Pierce would be the first to say he wasn't a sales star at ADM Labs. There was simply too much product chasing too few buyers. After a couple of weeks, they gave Pierce the database for folks who had contacted them previously, and he thought that might pan out a bit. It didn't. In the meantime, cubicles in the bullpen were being occupied and abandoned on a daily basis. After a month, they gave Pierce the entire smokeable hemp portfolio. As he deadpanned: "Seniority comes fast in the Hemp Space."

Nico, Pierce's boss, was tall, slim, exceptionally charismatic, and at home in nice suits. He came from Queens, New York, and had worked previously as a private concierge. "It's like this: I worked in a luxury lifestyle network. You want a white tiger for your kid's birthday party? A flight to Bermuda on an hour's notice? A pig that sniffs out truffles? That was me. I got to know a lot of professional sports figures, hedge fund guys, rich South Americans. It was an eye-opening experience for a kid from the outer boroughs. One of my clients asked me one day about CBD. I'd never heard of it. He said he was going into the business in Denver and would I be interested. I spent a week researching CBD, which wasn't easy back then. CBD hadn't yet popped, but looked like it might, so I signed on.

"I moved to Denver, and we started ADM Labs. Our mantra was 'Trust, loyalty, transparency.' We didn't really know exactly what part of CBD we'd be in. We leased a building and started visiting extraction labs and farms. I remember my first visit to a hemp farm. I was wearing a three piece suit with a pocket square. To me that was serious business attire in New York and certainly the attire for a private concierge with a client from Miami looking to get a cigarette boat with a Barnum & Bailey circus clown driving it for his daughter's *quinceañera*. That New York look didn't go over well in Colorado. The hemp farmers wouldn't even talk to me. They probably thought I was a character from *Goodfellas*. My name doesn't help, I suppose. After that I stopped wearing a tie.

"The labs we visited were unbelievable. Guys operating $200,000 machines sucking DMT with vape pens, everyone smoking joints, no safety protocols, and inventory control was a Sharpie mark on the door of a freezer. You might scoff at me being a private concierge, but let me tell you, it takes professionalism, tact, organizational skills, and a lot of creative thinking to be successful. These labs had none of those things, but they had demand for hemp. They didn't need a sales department. There was hardly any product available back then and whoever could supply oil or flower would just answer the phone and ship it.

"That was good, not bad. We knew how to properly operate a business. We saw there was a dirty side and a clean side to hemp. Extracting oil with methane or CO_2, or growing on a farm, was the dirty side. I mean this only in the context of requiring lots of permits and equipment. The clean side was post processing into various types of products consumer companies wanted. Hemp isolate, distillate, infused oils. We'd need a lab for that, but we wouldn't need fire suppression systems and special licenses. We thought a customer-based enterprise, well capitalized, with professional management, would thrive. We did. In 2018 we were coining money putting together buyers and sellers. We had twenty-five people on staff, but we wanted more than just that. We wanted hemp to become a legitimate industry. We joined the governor's Colorado Hemp Advancement and Management Plan initiative, and my partner was named vice chairman. We supported political candidates with donations and information. We were high-profile. The Hemp Space did in eighteen months what it might take a regular industry five or ten years to develop."

Nico was operating in the *real* Hemp Space, versus the CDA and hemp wannabe world. The CDA, in their few-and-far-between communications on the actual financials of hemp growing, had made it abundantly clear that hemp farmers should sign a contract ahead of time with a seller or processor to handle their crop. The reality was that there were only two ways to go. The first one was to sign a contract for some poundage of crop at some agreed price with some entity, and the other was to keep your cheeks in the wind and see what prices evolved after harvest. Both strategies backfired because when prices went to zero, the folks who had contracts found that the company they had contracted with had disappeared, gone bankrupt, or just refused to pay. It's kept the lawyers busy, but you can't squeeze blood from a stone. The folks who'd kept their cheeks in the wind were equally adrift, but at least they didn't go through the season thinking they had some kind of price that disappeared at the first sign of trouble.

Pierce enjoyed the buzz and personalities at ADM Labs. Everyone was working side deals. One had an indoor grow in New Mexico, another was working some angle with Amish hemp growers in Pennsylvania, another had a cattle ranch in Fort Lupton. At the desk next to Pierce was a New York hipster working on a drone that spread pesticides and a seed genetic with high Delta 8 THC. Some of the guys were into cryptocurrencies and one worked part-time in hot air balloon recapture. This motley crew was supervised by a tall Californian with waist-length dreadlocks. He always wore shorts that revealed his leg tattoos and parked his black Escalade in the handicapped space on the days he showed up. He supplemented his ADM sales manager salary as a Long Drive golf competitor and bullion trader. He also bought and sold IOS apps.

Pierce was initially impressed with all this entrepreneurial zeal until I pointed out that someone with a real business didn't have a dozen irons in the fire. They worked the iron that produced revenue. Not one of these folks was making it, and the more gigs somebody talked about the more I knew the whole thing was a sham. I'm sure it was the same in the Denver taverns in 1860 when the gold prospector came to town talking about his claim, or the Exxon executive in Grand Junction talking about shale oil, or the Arapahoe warrior talking about all his ponies. There wasn't much gold in them thar hills, Exxon had pulled out, and the Arapahoe had to eat his ponies who were starving for lack of winter forage. Nobody was buying or selling any hemp either. Colorado! Same as it ever was.

Pierce worked it hard. He's a born networker. I don't know how many events he attended rubbing elbows with other hempsters. He even joined the CHAMP working group which was started by Governor Polis and sought to "define a well-structured and defined supply chain for hemp in order to establish a strong market for the state's farming communities [by] seeking regulatory and industry subject matter experts to serve as stakeholder champions and help formulate Colorado's blueprint for hemp."

Pierce certainly qualified as a hemp expert and stakeholder champion. After all, he'd spent two and a half months drying and trimming plants. He'd gone home every day, stopped on the porch, peeled off his pants and stood them in a corner. Then he'd beeline to the shower. Hemp resin is sticky stuff and a day on the scaffolds spreads a defiant film over everything. You can change your clothes, but you can't get it all off yourself when you're handling hemp plants every day. Now that I think about it, this may have had something to do with my banking problems. Like Pigpen from *Peanuts*, who always had a cloud of dust around him, I had a cloud of hemp aroma around me everywhere I went. In retrospect, I probably should have used the drive-up window.

Pierce had earned additional hemp-expert spurs with his whole month in hemp sales. Between trimming and selling he had more experience than many folks at the CHAMP meetings. He discovered how one individual, just by regularly attending meetings, might exert some influence. In the final CHAMP report sent to the governor, he'd managed to excise any language about licensing requirements for drying, bucking, and trimming. I'm not sure if that's quite democracy, but it is effective.

But Pierce didn't sell a single bud the whole time he worked his cubicle at ADM Labs. Neither did anyone else, as far as he could tell. Pierce stuck it out, watching as one by one the desks and computers on the once bustling trading floor were dumped into an unused storage room down in the basement. When the coffee company came to repossess the espresso machine, he knew it was quitting time.

So Pierce turned to working from home and became a free agent. We still had a barn full of our own hemp to sell. He was calling and re-calling every single person he'd run across in the months he'd been immersed in the Hemp Space. He'd kept track of every contact he'd made in his Salesforce program, and the list was impressive. Between the CHAMP meetings, local meetups, someone who knew someone, and his time at ADM Labs, he had hundreds of prospects. The pitch was always the same: "How's it going? . . . I know . . . We're in the same boat . . . It's very disappointing . . . Got any leads on buyers?"

This was a slog, but not unlike his previous job.

His first sale was to a guy who bought ten pounds of hemp flower at $100 per pound. That was promising. The buyer wanted his purchase delivered, so Pierce loaded the bag into his beater Toyota and met the buyer in the back lot of a truck stop in Denver. Pierce circled the lot looking for a parked car with the brights on. When he got the arranged sign, he pulled in next to him. The buyer gave the bag a sniff and handed over ten Ben Franklins.

Whatever glamor Pierce and I had attached to the Hemp Space was fading fast.

Chapter 11
HERE COME THE COPS

P ierce's tireless phone calls began to bear a little fruit. There was a slow trickle of interest, and a slower trickle of buyers. Ten pounds here, twenty pounds there. We had thousands of pounds of totally legal hemp flower to sell, and at this pace it was going to take forever. Most of our buyers were from out of state and, at the beginning, we'd ship the product via FedEx. We didn't consider the US Postal Service because we figured that a quasi-federal enterprise would be hostile to hemp shipments. More often than not, our FedEx shipments were seized as suspected marijuana. They must have dogs at their facilities, or some smart machine. Smart enough to smell the hemp, maybe, but not smart enough (who is?) to distinguish legal hemp from MJ. Since we always shipped our product with a current Certificate of Analysis and our phone number and address, we were easy to find. We were legit and had nothing to hide. The first time our FedEx shipment was seized, Pierce tracked it down to a facility in Lexington, Kentucky. When asked the status of the shipment, he was put on hold by the representative there and then transferred to a supervisor. The supervisor eventually gave him the phone number for the on-site Kentucky detective who'd been assigned to investigate drug trafficking at this FedEx facility.

When Pierce called him, it was, initially, a frosty exchange.

"This is Pierce Grogan from Front Range Hemp Harvesting Services in Colorado. I hear you might be holding my shipment. Can we talk?"

"Glad you called, dirtbag. Saved me a bunch of shoe leather. You're in very deep doodoo."

"I called because I'm not a dirtbag, sir. I shipped legal hemp and am trying to get it to my customer."

"There's no such thing as legal hemp in Kentucky. We sent your stuff up to Frankfort for testing. Forty pounds of dope shipped interstate. That's so federal it's sick. When we get it back, I'll hand your case over to the US Attorney. We work together a lot and I like to make deposits in the favor bank. You're probably looking at forty years for your forty pounds."

"If I thought that was true, do you think I'd be calling you? Why would I do that?"

"Because people are dumb. Especially dope dealers."

"We're not dope dealers. Let's not argue the point. Can I send you some information from Senator McConnell's office? You know who Mitch McConnell is, right?"

"Don't try and be funny. Everyone in Kentucky knows Mitch."

"I'm not trying to be funny at all. I'm scared to death. I want to clear this up. Senator McConnell's the guy who legalized hemp, and not just in Kentucky. You need a license to handle hemp flower, which is what I sent. We have the proper license and so does the consignee. They'd be happy to send you a copy."

"OK, I'll play along. I know where you are and I'm just waiting for the lab test before the DEA comes for you. Send me whatever you want."

"Thank you."

Pierce sent off a copy of the USDA Farm Bill, the revised Kentucky hemp statutes, and a couple of newspaper articles to the detective. Pierce waited a day and called him back.

"You got the materials?"

"Yeah. You could have made it all up. But I did some digging of my own. The world changes fast. I didn't know about all this hemp shit. I'm here to interdict drugs. Your stuff looks like drugs, smells like drugs, and as far as I know, still is drugs, but I appreciate your phone calls."

This was every hemp grower's nightmare. Nobody wanted to get dragged into America's war on drugs. Our shipping problems were a perfect illustration of our government's hostility to hemp and our entire society's schizophrenia regarding drug use. Like most of my countrymen, I hadn't paid much attention to the drug wars. I only got interested when I entered the Hemp Space and had to get a fast education on THC limits. That made me wonder why hemp became legal in 2018, which led me into wondering why it had become illegal in 1937.

———

Both hemp and marijuana go under the moniker *Cannabis sativa*. The essential difference between the two is the quantity of THC within any given plant.

Use of cannabis has been traced to Asia, as fiber and food, as far back as 12,000 BCE, and for smoking to around 2,500 BCE. Nobody's sure how cannabis came to North America, but hemp for rope, clothing fiber, and sails for ships and was certainly grown from colonial times. The word "canvas" comes from cannabis with a direct line to the Anglo-French word *chanevaz,* meaning made from hemp. This was, presumably, not the stuff you smoked to get high.

Marijuana, and by extension hemp, became illegal in 1937 shortly after Harry J. Anslinger was named head of the Federal Bureau of Narcotics, which had succeeded the Bureau of Prohibition and eventually became the Drug Enforcement Administration (DEA).

The use of narcotics, a federal definition which still includes cannabis, was not a prevalent public health problem when the Federal Bureau of Narcotics was established in 1930. Indeed, the agency's budget had been cut in half between 1930 and 1934. In 1932 Anslinger considered marijuana "an inconsequential nuisance." By 1935 something had shifted and Anslinger launched a massive campaign to indoctrinate the nation on the dangers of marijuana. His campaign was enthusiastically supported by the Hearst newspaper chain, always eager to foment racial tension, and by the cotton industry, which viewed hemp fiber as an undesirable competitor.

The 1930s was also the decade when the treatment of people addicted to narcotics was shifted from the medical system to the judicial system. The medical view of addiction was replaced by the bigoted and erroneous notion that people addicted to drugs were morally impoverished, potentially dangerous, and in any case mostly Black or Latino. This shift marked the beginning of the drug wars in America.

It's important to understand that what is so often called our War on Drugs is actually multiple wars fought on very different fronts. There is the war by federal law enforcement to keep drugs from getting into the country, including extra-territorial interventions in places like Colombia, Panama, Mexico, and

Peru. There is the federal war against money laundering by transnational cartels. There is the internal policy war between the DEA and people in the hemp space on THC limits. Then there are the various wars conducted by local and federal law enforcement against criminals who sell drugs in particular places, against people who commit crimes to obtain drugs, against people who recreationally use drugs, and against people who are addicted to drugs.

By 1973, when the Federal Bureau of Narcotics became the DEA, the Nixon administration had doubled down on drug interdiction and prosecution. Nixon was the first to use the term "War on Drugs" and called drug abuse Public Enemy Number One. Ronald Reagan went even further in the 1980s by increasing mandatory prison terms for nonviolent drug offenders and supporting Nancy Reagan's "Just Say No" campaign with billions of federal dollars. Today the USA incarcerates more people per capita than any OECD country by a long margin. Of the 2.3 million Americans in jails and prisons, one in five are in for nonviolent drug offenses.

This is appalling.

I'm not some dreadlocked hippie, nor am I a drug user. I'm a sixty-five-year-old small business owner, family farmer, retired truck driver, and, in the not too distant past, elected public official. I'm inside the system, and I'm horrified.

One of the many tragic side dramas of the War on Drugs has been the vilification of any citizen, politician, health worker, or law enforcement professional looking to explore the outcomes of our drug policies. They can expect immediate condemnation by the drug warriors and be forever branded as "soft on drugs," a label which, if imputed upon you, amounts to nothing less than professional annihilation. The drug warriors have controlled the narrative and ensured that any rational discussion on the efficacy of the drug wars remains unthinkable. That influence is fading, but not fast enough.

A point the drug warriors prefer not to stress is that most drug users are not addicts or dangerous. Substance addiction is a serious medical problem and should be treated that way, but drug use is simply a creative approach to changing one's state of mind or body through an outside agent. It's a solid thread running through the entire history of *Homo sapiens*. Alcohol, sugar, caffeine, tobacco, cannabis, pharmaceuticals, and other substances are all used to make us feel some other way than we do at a given moment. It's as basic to the human impulse as thirst or sex and has run through all cultures throughout time. The desire to change one's current state doesn't even require a drug. It can be as simple as running in circles to get dizzy, performing a religious rite, or even something as benign as meditation.

That doesn't always get you there, though, so *Homo sapiens* found plants that would: grapes, hops, potatoes, apples, betel nuts, qat, coffee, coca leaves, mushrooms, sugar cane, cacao, poppies, cannabis, and cactus, to name just a few. We also invented drugs: Valium, Demerol, thalidomide, codeine, Seconal, Thorazine, Xoloft, Percocet, Lexapro, Vicodin, Ritalin, Adderal, Xanax, Paxil, Prozac, ketamine, Wellbutrin, fentanyl, morphine, heroin, Oxycodone, LSD, methamphetamine, Meprobamate, Celexa, Cymbalta, Effexor, Lortab, Oxycontin, Percodan, Methaqualone, Dexedrine, mescaline, and MDMA. This is an abbreviated list, and of the thirty-four drugs listed here, only two are completely illegal.

I regularly use caffeine, sugar, acetaminophen, aspirin, chocolate, diphenhydramine, alcohol, theobromine, CBD, naproxen, nicotine, phenylephrine, amlodipine besylate, and ibuprofen. That's fourteen drugs, and I don't think anyone would consider me a drug user. The truth is, we're all drug users. In the US, prescriptions for just Zoloft and Lexapro amount to over 64 million per year. Xanax is 26 million.

When I look at this from a compassionate side, I might wonder why so many people take drugs to change their current experience. I often wonder why I do so myself. We all have our psychological and/or physical pain and sometimes we just want it to go away for a while. I don't see that as a moral failing, I see it as a humanitarian concern. I also see it as strictly personal business.

Prohibiting any of these things has always proved to be a game of Whack-a-Mole. Alcohol prohibition lasted thirteen years when it was finally given up as hopeless, while the drug wars have been going on for a century. One of the key differences is that the money to be made from illegal drugs was and is orders of magnitude greater. A central theme of *The Godfather* is who is going to profit from this new business of drug trafficking and which criminal syndicate will eventually prevail. We know the answer to that now. In real life, they all prevailed. Since 1971 the federal government has spent over a trillion dollars fighting illegal drugs. In the meantime, Americans' use of illegal and legal drugs has ballooned, while transnational drug cartels have become sovereign shadow states. Let's toss in the corruption (as if it needed more) of the global financial system by drug money. Those results alone have caused many people to change their minds about the War on Drugs. That the drug wars also resulted in a disproportionate share of drug arrests and imprisonment of people of color has had a massive destabilizing effect on absolutely everything in our society. This system of sending nonviolent drug offenders to prison has long been known in minority communities, with many people from those communities shouting from the rooftops since at least the 1940s that we were creating a gulag archipelago right here in the land of the free.

I'll go even further by positing that we've been looking at the problem in reverse from the very beginning. Drug addiction is not usually a major problem for an entire society. It's definitely a problem for the addict, but that's different. In the USA, we've been told that street crime, overdoses, emergency room visits, crime syndicates, money laundering, prostitution, police corruption, prison overcrowding, not enough cops, overflowing court dockets, and gang violence are all the horrific consequences of drug addiction. These serious problems have nothing at all to do with addiction. They are all caused by interdiction.

If you can allow that counterintuitive viewpoint in for just a moment, the whole Gordian knot of the drug war dissolves. It's the crimes people perpetrate in response to drug *scarcity* that are the problem. Addicts aren't particularly dangerous to anyone but themselves, unless their drugs are scarce and expensive. When that happens, addicts do become a truly menacing and dangerous antisocial force. Their quest for whatever drug they're addicted to also spawns the criminals who work for the cartels that supply it. It's an easy connection, after you've accepted the basic premise, to realize that the government's drug warriors created this mess.

Of course, the recreational use of drugs contributes mightily to the crimes perpetrated by the cartels and their minions. On examination, though, our current differentiation of the relative danger of various drugs makes no sense. Many drugs like alcohol, nicotine, sugar, and caffeine, are, for various cultural reasons, legal. Other drugs, also for cultural reasons, are illegal. The legality or illegality of any drug is hardly ever related to its objective social or medical danger. If they were, alcohol, by any measure, would win the race by miles. Cheers!

———

In Kentucky, FedEx kept stopping our shipments and handing them over to the authorities. It happened so often that Pierce and the detective became sort of friendly on the phone.

"Hey Pierce, I'm calling again from Lexington. We've got another one of yours. Got anything to tell me?"

"Yessir. Same story. Hemp under 0.3%, grown in Boulder, Colorado, destined this time for South Carolina. You've got the COA. South Carolina's a Delta 9 only state. You can test it. It's solid."

"We're not going to test it. I have two hundred more calls to make. You make it easy by putting your phone number on the shipping documents so you're always my first call. The others take some digging. I always find 'em, but it's a pain in my ass. I think you're legit, or as legit as anyone is in this mess. I wonder sometimes if I pissed off my boss somehow and he gave me this assignment to torture me. If he did, it's working."

"I know the feeling. My boss makes me put *my* name and phone number on all these shipments. That's why I'm talking to you instead of him."

"I feel like a blind man trying to find his dog on the infield at the Derby. I don't like being confused. What's all this lingo? COA? Delta 9?"

"How much time do you have? I'd be happy to give you Hemp 101, but it's complicated."

"It sounds complicated, but I have no time. My whole day is making calls like this. Not quite like this. This is almost a conversation. Nobody told me jack about hemp on this assignment. You try and keep up with all the crap we have to . . . Forget about the laws. We got sensitivity training, continuing education, and for some reason, Kentucky decided to start a war about who's supposed to use which bathroom. You should see the toilet memos we get. It's impossible to stay current."

"We have just one porta-potty for everyone here on the farm. It simplifies things a lot. I'll tell you one thing: regardless of how anyone identifies their gender, they all use toilet paper. Lots of it. More than you'd ever think."

"Now you're trying to be funny. Thanks for trying to make my day better and letting me let off some steam. Truth is, I haven't sent your boxes off to the lab. They're so backed up; it'll take months to test. Have your consignees send their license to me. If the license looks legit, now that I know they're supposed to have one, and now that I know what the license is supposed to look like, I'll see what I can do."

"You're sure? They're kind of nervous about this."

"I won't bust 'em."

"I'm sorry you're in this position, sir. I really am. We are legit, or as legit anyone is in this mess. I appreciate you calling rather than sending out a SWAT team."

"Nobody's sending out SWAT teams over hemp shipments. The truth is, we local guys hate all this. Hemp, weed, so what? People are gonna use this stuff. It's not good for them, I'm sure about that, but I'm a trained investigator and there are lots of very bad people out there doing worse things. We should be apprehending them before they do serious violence to regular people. This is a waste of my time and experience. I spend my whole day grabbing hemp shipments that turn out to be legal commerce. The DEA guys are pressing us hard but I'm not a fed. The feds are insane about this. They say, 'Grab everything coming from Colorado!' It makes no sense. Legalize the shit! It'll keep the money away from the cartels, and if people die, well, they're dying anyway. Let me do the job I want to do, which is catching bad guys. Not this."

"So you'll release my shipment?"

"I'm not a decision-maker anymore. Different department now. The DEA revoked local autonomy. I'm just a mid-level shit-shoveler now. You should probably kiss your shipment goodbye and be grateful. You're lucky it's me at this desk instead of some whipper-snapper trying to make a career. I'm a jaded lifer. Why don't you use the US Postal Service like all the other dope dealers?"

"We're not dope dealers."

"Right. I forgot. What *you* need to forget is Federal Express. Local detectives like me don't care about hemp, or even marijuana, being sent to other states. But FedEx cares a lot. That's why they're grabbing all your stuff. They see a Colorado package and off it goes to the sniffers."

"I've wondered about that. How do they figure it out? Do they use dogs, camels, hungry college students wanting free weed?"

"We can't go into our methods . . ."

"Let me be sure I have this right: you're suggesting I use the quasi-federal government postal service to ship product the feds hate and not use the private sector which is legally allowed to ship this product."

"Bingo."

"Thanks for the tip. We'll do that."

"You're welcome. I hope I don't have to call you again. I enjoy talking with you but it's still a waste of my time."

"Take care, sir. Nothing personal here, but I don't want to talk to you again either."

So much for the war on drugs from a non-DEA investigator on the ground. A boring, stupid waste of time that prevents them from catching real criminals.

These communications with our detective friend kept us from getting arrested, but it didn't help our shipments. They weren't getting through to the buyers. Buyers always paid in advance, so a seized shipment meant returning their money and fighting with FedEx to get our product back. We never did get any product back. As a former trucker who's spent more time in large warehouses than I care to brood about, I've got a pretty good idea where those shipments ended up. Enjoy smoking that hemp you took home, Mr. Forklift Driver. It's not gonna get you high, though.

The weird irony was that it was true that only the US Postal Service allowed hemp shipments through on a regular basis. We were figuring it out. Our guy in South Carolina called someone he knew who called someone he knew and then we had two more customers. Still, the pace of sales was excruciatingly slow. In addition to selling off the hemp flower, we had to sell off our biomass trim and all the processing equipment. We were dumping everything. Those sales were completely different. The biomass buyers were extractors, and they had a clear sense of the market. The year before, biomass was selling at $80 per pound; Pierce sold our entire stock for $2 per pound. This was prime hemp trim that had cost $62 per pound to produce and we considered ourselves lucky to get two bucks. I could have cried. We even had to deliver it in a U-Haul truck which smelled like hemp when we picked it up and smelled even more like hemp when we dropped it off. Every U-Haul truck in Colorado smelled like hemp that year. At least my barn was emptying out.

The machinery buyers were all growers. As June went into July, Pierce started to get serious callbacks for our buckers, trimmers, fans, generators, snippers, gloves, and everything else. This was déjà vu for us. All the growers were figuring out, just a few weeks before harvest, that they'd need specialized equipment to turn their crop into flower. Hadn't they talked to anyone about what happened the year before? Obviously not. In a few weeks Pierce sold off every piece of equipment we had, right down to the last extension cord. One of our potential buyers was none other than Alec Solimeo, the hemp farmer next door to the weedwhackers. Alec had landed a gig as farm manager for another hemp crop, again, just up the road. We liked Alec and wanted him to get our stuff. This farm was owned by a guy who owned several hundred pizza franchises in Russia. The Kommissar started questioning our pricing and thought he could bargain. By the time he figured out it was a seller's market, everything was gone.

As Alec told me in a resigned tone, "This is how they learn."

Chapter 12
LAST CALL

With all the equipment sales, we were getting to know growers all over Colorado. Nobody had any more idea about where they were going to sell their product than they had the year before. This boded well for our budding brokerage business. We figured that after we sold off our own flower, we could tap into a direct pipeline to hundreds of acres of other farmers. This encouraged us a lot. Even at $60 per pound, smokeable flower could make money for a broker, if not for the grower. The standard commission was 10%, so if Pierce sold 1,000 pounds of flower, that was $60,000 gross and carried a $6,000 commission. Do one of these a month and it's almost a real business. Do a couple a month and it's a cash machine.

One of these promising supply prospects was Sanh Ho, from way out in northeastern Colorado. That's where the really big hemp farms were. Companies like Colorado Cultivars were boasting 4,000 acres of hemp under cultivation in Eaton. Down south, in the San Luis Valley, there were even larger grows. These guys were growing strictly for biomass. When we were processing, we'd tried to convince some of them to give us their colas to turn into smokeable flower product, but they weren't interested. We now knew that all their buds had been seeded by male pollen from nearby farms and the colas weren't worth processing.

Pierce unearthed Sanh Ho from somewhere deep in his mining efforts for hemp growers to buy our equipment. Sanh came to our farm to buy a Triminator. It was one of our more pleasant experiences. Sanh was Vietnamese and showed up with his whole family. It looked to me to be an outing, or maybe they came en masse for security, but it didn't feel that way. After Sanh handed Pierce ten grand in cash, we loaded the Triminator, brand-new and still in its crate, using my tractor, and lashed it down using my moving van straps. Loading finished, we all paused for a moment. Sanh saw the pack of American Spirits sitting on the checkout desk near the barn door and tipped his head in that direction in an interrogatory gesture. This was a familiar ritual to old salts like me who'd spent time in Asia and Eastern Europe before 1989, when sharing cigarettes was considered the friendliest of social gestures.

"I'm sorry," I said, "I've been impolite. Please." I picked up the pack and offered it to the group. They all took one, one of the guys took two. I lit them all and fired up one for myself. This was Old World protocol. Everyone then leaned against the loaded truck, apparently in no hurry, and took a few drags. Sanh looked around.

"Nice place here," he said. "How much?" Manuel, our Mexican fixer, could have pulled a page from our new Asian friend in verbal directness.

"1.2 million."

"Too much. Land cheaper out east. You got water?"

"All I need."

"Water big problem out east."

"Not here."

"Why you not grow hemp here?"

"Too many growers."

"Too many growers not the problem. Too many pollen makers. Make seed. Bad product."

"How do you handle that out east? There are huge growers out there."

"All inside."

"Inside?"

"All inside. Seventeen hoophouses."

"Growing for smokeable flower?"

"All flower. No profit in biomass."

Sanh Ho didn't have a seeding problem because he was growing indoors, which is where the whole industry was quickly moving. Rogue male plants are a plague that gets worse every year and indoor growing allows for year-round cultivation and a steady stream of product. Indoor growing isn't agriculture, though; it's high-tech, high-capital hydroponics. Soon there won't be any outdoor hemp grown in Colorado at all. So much for hemp helping Colorado farmers reverse the trend of bankruptcies. Still, I was very curious about where someone might sell all that bud. It was the Holy Grail, and I tried to sound casual when I asked Sanh:

"Where do you sell your flower?"

"Ah, now, there problem." He stole another look at the pack of American Spirits, and I served up another round. He continued: "Where you sell your flower?"

"We're trying to figure that out."

"We too. Price very good two year before. Our small family move here from San Diego. Grow hemp. Larger big family. Everyone agree, we come. Everyone give money. Make big profit, they say."

"Since you're all indoor, how much product could you produce every month?"

"With new Triminator, one thousand pounds, every week. We good growers, not so good selling. Big problem. Big problem with big family."

"Maybe we could sell some of your product?"

"Sound good. Like that. Talk soon. Thanks for smoke. Bye."

Holy Toledo! Besides former marijuana dealers, Boomers, and scientists, apparently Vietnamese speculators were pooling their money in California and sending families a thousand miles east to grow hemp. But where to sell it?

This was the central problem for Sanh Ho and everyone else. He had seventeen hoophouses in which he was growing smokeable flower. He could easily supply 1,000 pounds a week year-round. What he couldn't do, what nobody could do, so far, was sell it. Just one fully equipped hoophouse costs at least $30,000, so Sanh and his extended family had easily spent over $500,000 for the hoophouses, and that didn't include the ground rent, electricity, and labor costs, which had to be well into six figures. And that didn't include water.

Water. Here's another huge difference between the West and the East Coast. Nobody back East even thinks about the cost of water. In Colorado, lots of people think about nothing else. A hookup to a water company in Connecticut might cost a $150 service fee. Out here, it's $62,000 for a residential connection. Commercial connections run well into six figures. Every drop out here is owned by someone. Even the drops that haven't fallen yet are already owned. You're not even allowed to collect the water from your own gutters when it rains.

I have a ditch running right through the middle of my farm but since I don't have water rights to it, woe to me if I even dip a coffee mug into it to water a blade of grass. These ditches aren't random troughs just lying around. They were built in the 1890s by ditch companies who went high up into the Rockies and diverted the mountain runoff onto the plains. The original settlers bought shares in these companies to ensure they'd have water for their farms. When later settlers began diverting the diversions, things got violent. They eventually arrived at an armistice with what's called the Law of Prior Appropriation. That means the first person to divert the water holds senior rights to it. This legal precept, also called "First in time, first in right" is a strictly Darwinian concept and still very much in effect. Ditch companies have a staffer called a ditch rider who's effectively a water policeman. Ditch rights supersede property rights, so the ditch rider can come onto my property any time. He can show up with a bulldozer to clean out the ditch if he feels like it without even telling me. There's an Old West adage: "Whiskey is for drinking and water is for fighting," and fight they do. Water law is a specialized field in Colorado and quite lucrative. In Denver alone, there are more than fifty law firms that specialize in nothing but water law. The lawyers get rich because proving "first in time" is a murky business, often with millions of dollars at stake. My farm has water rights from a different ditch at the northern end of the property, not close to the pastures, so I have a Rube Goldberg system of pipes to get my water to where it needs to be. That the other ditch I can't use runs right through my pastures is maddening, particularly so since the water itself comes from the same reservoir where I have shares.

Water rights are bought and sold on the open market and lots of rights are owned by hedge funds. It can be a good investment. One of my neighbors bought up a bunch of water shares in the 1950s for $30 a share. Now they're selling for $4,500 a share. You can rent your shares by the season so there's income, too. I can't even imagine Sanh Ho's water bills out there on the plains keeping 200,000 hemp plants happy.

Knowing that Sanh Ho could supply 1,000 pounds of hemp flower a week fitted nicely into our brokering plans. And Sanh Ho wasn't our only supply source. Pierce and I figured we could play the growers off one another and sell the product from the grower willing to take the lowest price. Instead of commission, we might even buy product on spec and sell it later for a better margin. After all, we had one of the only truly climate-controlled storage spaces for hemp in Colorado.

This was energizing, and Pierce redoubled his efforts to find the demand side. That wasn't energizing at all. We had some customers, mostly CBD shops, but smokeable flower wasn't their main business and ten pounds was, for them, a huge buy. Besides, the CBD shops were being flooded with sales calls from farmers desperate to sell flower. Flower was sold by a guy who knew a guy. It was a wispy cirrus cloud that appeared and disappeared in a whirlwind of contacts, shifting alliances, and occasional benevolence. It was a buyer's market and not big enough for us to make a business, especially since the CBD stores were closing almost as fast as they opened.

We held on through the summer, working the phones, thinking there had to be some large buyer somewhere looking for hemp flower in bulk. There must be! All these growers, like Sanh Ho, were producing tons of flower. It had to be going somewhere.

It *was* going somewhere.

Pierce's phone calls were working their way through mycological filaments of the Hemp Space. We started to get an increasing ooze of buyers coming to the farm. These weren't shopkeepers or extractors. These were shady, quiet men, driven in cars, apparently not their own, for they invariably got out on the passenger side, leaving the driver fixed at the wheel. These men, always men, had no chitchat. They eschewed the usual introductory conversations inside the Hemp Space, which were invariably about prices, growing season challenges, and the USDA Interim Final Rule. These guys would grunt a greeting, look at the buds, smell them, and not one of them ever asked for a COA.

One morning I received an early knock on my door. Pierce hadn't mentioned any appointments. I opened the door, slightly apprehensive but not totally paranoid.

"I'm Ace. I just flew in from Dallas on the early plane and rented a car. I hear you have hemp flower for sale."

"Who'd you hear that from?"

"Not sure. Somebody from somewhere, I guess."

"Let's go out to the barn."

"Let's."

I knew better than to ask any more questions. I showed him the bins full of buds.

"Open any of them. Take a random sample. It's all from the same farm."

He opened about ten of them, examined the buds and sniffed them a bit.

"We'll take fifteen hundred pounds at sixty dollars a pound."

"Sounds fine."

"I have to make some calls. The wire transfer will come through in a couple hours."

"Why don't you come inside? I've got some coffee going."

"I'll wait in the car."

Come inside for coffee! What a chump I was. I was still thinking this was some sort of normal business transaction with regular people. The social niceties were neither required nor desired in this environment. Sure enough, the wire came in before noon for $90,000. Shortly thereafter, a Mercedes Sprinter van, black of course, showed up. Ace did the weighing and loading. The driver was a Russian or Bulgarian who spoke no English or pretended he didn't. He leaned against the Sprinter and smoked one Gauloise after another in quiet repose. Apparently, drivers didn't load. He reminded me of certain van line truck drivers who cultivated indolence with an impressive and insolent perfection.

After Ace put the 1,500 pounds into the van, they all vaporized. I didn't know Ace, didn't know the ultimate buyer, and certainly didn't know the mute driver. This farm with the hemp storage barn was also my home. I felt invaded and filthy, but not filthy enough to halt the transaction. I'd lost enough money and $90,000 was too much for me to waste any effort navelgazing about the moral high ground. Besides, it was a perfectly legal transaction.

At long last, the Case of the Disappearing Smokeable Flower had been solved. Sherlock Holmes, a famous drug user himself, nicotine and cocaine being his favorites, would have figured it out much earlier with half an ounce of shag and a few scratches on his violin. Pierce and I were more obtuse, but we finally got it. There *was* no legitimate market for smokeable hemp flower. My old buddy from the Hemp Growers Association had hinted at this way back when he told me, "There's a lot more market interaction between marijuana and hemp than people think." That was a very diplomatic way of putting it.

Hemp flower was being bought to mix in with marijuana by dealers not overly concerned with repeat business. The economics of marijuana dealing make the point obvious. A pound of marijuana bud sells for about $1,600, a pound of hemp bud for $60. Just like a heroin dealer is going to cut his stock with talcum powder, baking soda, or, in nasty cases, rat poison to increase profit margins, a marijuana dealer is going to cut his pound of weed with some hemp, or just spray some Delta 8 THC onto the hemp buds. This is easy to do because, other than the fact that hemp flower doesn't get you high, it's impossible to tell the difference between a hemp bud and a marijuana bud unless you have an organic chemistry setup and a few hours to kill. It looks the same, feels the same, and smells the same whether raw or burned. No doubt some hemp sommeliers will claim they can always tell the difference, but if that's true, they're as rare as home chemical setups. The customers in our fledgling brokerage business were exclusively marijuana dealers and they were all our bigger-volume buyers, with a legit CBD shop or two on the fringe.

While we certainly could have made that a business, since there is no end-user certificate required for hemp flower and we had unlimited supply, neither Pierce nor I had the stomach for it. We'd been telling everyone for a year we weren't dope dealers. It wasn't just greed, after all. Maybe we'd drank more of the hemp kombucha than we thought. We were different, and hemp was different. Maybe CBD will be the new wonder drug. If it is, it's going to be from indoor-grown plants to make biomass for full-spectrum CBD. The hemp flower space was a dirty business, and we wanted no part of it.

So, Pierce and I began the laborious process of shutting down, which paradoxically meant ramping up. We had almost nobody left working for us now except a couple of guys on a part-time basis burping the bins and doing some last-minute hand trimming. Pierce was sticking with me now out of loyalty and honor. He was determined to get as much lost money as possible back to me. He, too, wanted to exit in an orderly fashion. That showed real character. He could have bolted anytime and left me with the mess.

———

Not long after we sold off our last flower, another big order taken away in another black Sprinter van, I got a phone call.

"Is this Front Range Hemp Harvesting Services?"

"Sort of."

"Billy Held said you might process our hemp crop."

"How's Billy?"

"I guess he's fine. I don't actually know him. He's kind of a connection through a connection. He said you guys were straight up. We're looking for someone to process our twenty acres of Colorado hemp into smokeable flower."

"My name is Finn Murphy. What's yours?"

"Ralph."

"Got a last name?"

"Snodsmith."

"Is this how this conversation is going to go? The real Ralph Snodsmith, the gardening guy on the radio, died in 2010. I can't imagine there are two people with that name, even in this big country."

"Sorry about that. I represent a hedge fund in Brooklyn. That's in New York."

"Oh, that Brooklyn. Thanks for the geography lesson. If you know anything about me, you already know that I know where every single town in America is. There are twenty Brooklyns in America. Twenty-four if you change the spelling a little."

"I don't know a thing about you."

"That seems a little strange, since you're calling me. What's a hedge fund?"

"A hedge fund is a targeted . . . Now you're playing with me.

Point to you. I respect that. I told you, we're looking for a post-harvest processor for our hemp crop. Billy said you guys were the best."

"We were."

"Not anymore?"

"We sold everything off. Nobody pays their bills in the Hemp Space."

"Hemp Space?"

"The hemp industry. You should have known that term."

"Point two to you. Here's the deal: we've assembled a tranche of investors who want to grow hemp flower as one discrete element in a multinational multidisciplinary long-term diversified investment portfolio that includes previously neglected emerging markets with a long-term view toward maximizing potential financial growth."

"Did you just say that whole thing without an inhale?"

"I did. That's the strategy. Hemp is more complicated than it looks. We need someone to process the plants. Did you know hemp flower sells for forty times the price of hemp biomass?"

"I've heard that. So, who buys this forty times biomass flower?"

"That's our problem. Can you do twenty acres for us?"

"I'd need to be paid up front. It'll be at least a million dollars."

"That's about what we figured. We won't pay you up front, but we will put $1 million in escrow with an attorney, payable upon delivery of approved product."

"You're a year late. We'd have jumped on this last September."

"Maybe you were a year early. You've got it all figured out now."

"You're right. We do have it all figured out now. We're not dope dealers."

"We're not either. We're a hedge fund. We're a targeted . . ."

"I know what you think you are. Maybe you don't know what you really are, maybe you do. Either way I don't care anymore."

"Can you recommend another processor?"

I hung up.

I felt clean, for the first time in a long time.

EPILOGUE

M y climate-controlled barn is now empty of hemp except for one orphan wardrobe carton with 50 or so pounds of prime hemp trim. I'm slowly getting rid of it, giving bags to friends or as tips to delivery drivers and various service providers. The bags are rarely refused. Hemp is firmly established here in Colorado as a quasi-currency.

Billy Held is going strong with his product line, his private sales channels, and his eight acres under hemp cultivation. Ryan Lynch is still selling his top-notch hemp seed, growing a few acres here and there, and supplying consumer brands with his clean product. Tom Ward planted again, too. He's selling his horse CBD online and seems pleased with the results. Colin Gallagher and Jake Salazar are still running Solari Hemp. I see their product everywhere. Nico Anthony and his partner rebranded ADM Labs into HempCorp. They're still at it. Alec Solimeo is out of the Hemp Space. He's back to running integrated farms. It pays no real money, but he's happier. Last time I saw him we chatted in his driveway while waiting for a tow company to seize his pickup truck. Sanh Ho abandoned his seventeen hoophouses in Eaton,

Colorado, and moved back with his family to San Diego. Last time I spoke with him, he said for me to call him in a year.

Manuel started his own roofing business with Francisco. Violent hailstorms are common out here and sometimes they do serious damage to roofs and cars. A roofing company connected to an insurance company had hired Francisco as a salesman because of his pleasant demeanor. Francisco found that he was very successful in the Longmont Latino community but less so in the more affluent areas. His in-person sales calls in the fancier neighborhoods more often resulted in him explaining to police what he was doing rather than earning commissions. He eventually realized that rather than wasting his sales skills working for the gringo, he and Manuel should partner up and forge their own deal with the insurance company. Hailstorms are an equal-opportunity cataclysm, after all. Manuel, for all his amazing skills, is no salesman. Not for himself nor anyone else. Francisco does the sales and Manuel does the roofs. They have an LLC, pay their taxes, pull building permits, and make a decent living. Give people a chance to overcome mistakes and they can find some kind of American dream. I wish them both well.

Pierce landed on his feet, as he always has. He's back in sales doing high-end real estate rentals. A step above where he was when I plucked him for the Hemp Space. He got married and bought a house in a town just south of Boulder. The house he bought had a desert in the backyard and he bought a bunch of sod and an irrigation system that he's installing himself.

"If you and I hadn't done hemp together, I'd be paying someone to do this. It's not that hard."

I really miss working with him. In all the time we worked together we never had a cross word between us. I loved that part of it. We built and ran that hemp factory, goddammit! Other than not getting paid, we were successful. Except we weren't. None of it counts without revenue. Every enterprise needs to produce more than it consumes. If it doesn't, the end result is starvation or thievery. There is no third way.

———

As for me, I had a blast in the Hemp Space. I started up a new venture, was privileged to work with my godson, and learned a boatload about hemp. When I finally totted up the numbers, I lost over $300,000 in thirteen months. After a dozen startups, I'm still ahead, but the hemp adventure lowered my batting average considerably. I'm not proud of that. I hate losing money in business and I've never lost anything close to that in any other business. Given my late age, it's disconcerting.

I still have the farm but am decidedly *not* shopping for granite barns from Pennsylvania to ship out here. I've got some cattle in the pastures that pay about $3,000 a year and chickens that pay with eggs. That's my revenue stream. It's so far from $100,000 an acre it's embarrassing to even mention it. I'll never grow hemp, but I might still adopt a couple of wild burros that would otherwise be shot by BLM Wildlife Services. I can give at least two of them, maybe more, a very nice home.

Every night I listen to the coyotes howling and enjoy the view down the Front Range and count my blessings. I think I'll stay here. Run a little ranch, restore some grassland, live a quiet life. I walk my dog over the fields every morning. She's a charming blue heeler rescue named Charley. She knows exactly what she wants. She wants a tennis ball to run after and the occasional Red Devon yearling to herd. She'll run that poor calf all over the field. I understand Charley. She's got herding skills but no clue about what to do with them in any productive way. Me too. I've been running at warp seven since I was eighteen. I've chased a lot of tennis balls myself, and herded people, nipping at their heels to make them do what I want, without any clearer sense of a destination than a dog.

That's unsettling, and I feel like I need to pay some penance for nipping at people's heels all those years. I spend a lot of my time as a volunteer instructor teaching skiing to people with disabilities at Eldora Mountain outside Boulder. It probably doesn't count as penance, though, because working with these folks, who have real challenges, isn't suffering at all—it's energizing.

Maybe that's all I need, but I'm not as smart as my blue heeler. I'm not entirely satisfied with such a simple and pleasurable journey. It's more likely I'll get some new idea about a business, and off I'll go.

The coyotes I listen to at night all live over on the giant Table Mountain scientific facility just to the east. It's owned and operated by the federal government. There are two massive radio telescopes on the property. Rumor has it that DARPA uses the facility to monitor drug trafficking communications.

Good luck with that, boys. Go chase those tennis balls.

I'm out.

ACKNOWLEDGMENTS

Thanks to all the great folks at W. W. Norton, who never forget that serious work doesn't mean there can't be fun. That goes especially for Matt Weiland, my wise editor.

I'm grateful to all the players in the Hemp Space who made themselves available for this book. Special appreciation goes to Nico Anthony, Colin Gallagher, Billy Held, Ryan Lynch, Craig Mays, Cameron Murdock, Dr. Ernest Small, Alec Solimeo, and Tom Ward.

I'm indebted to Reid Page, Ted Biderman, Meghan Hungate, Greg Ellis, and Rochonne Sanchez for excellent professional advice that sometimes I even took.

On the writing end, thanks to Christopher Hunt, Cullen Murphy, and Philip Glouchevitch.

To my agent Rafe Sagalyn, who doesn't seem to mind slumming with me on the fringes of the American dream.

To Lisa Trank for all the handholding, and Deb who doesn't roll her eyes when I repair to the barn to write.

To my nephew, godson, business partner, and alter ego, Pierce Grogan. Thanks for putting your cheeks into the wind with me on this.

ALSO AVAILABLE FROM FINN MURPHY

A NATIONAL BESTSELLER

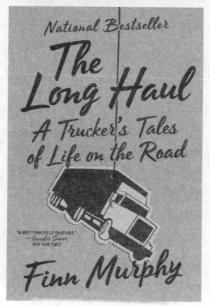

"Almost shamefully enjoyable."
—Jennifer Senior, *New York Times*

"There's nothing semi about Finn Murphy's trucking
tales of *The Long Haul*."
—Sloane Crosley, *Vanity Fair*

"Like a Mark Twain behind the wheel, [Finn Murphy] takes us on the
road coast to coast and city to city with a voice that's honest and direct
and sometimes even poetic."
—Bob Ryan, *Boston Globe*

W. W. NORTON & COMPANY
Independent Publishers Since 1923